THE LAYMAN'S BIBLE COMMENTARY

THE LAYMAN'S BIBLE COMMENTARY
IN TWENTY-FIVE VOLUMES

THE LAYMAN'S
BIBLE COMMENTARY

Balmer H. Kelly, *Editor*

Donald G. Miller   *Associate Editors*   Arnold B. Rhodes

Dwight M. Chalmers, *Editor, John Knox Press*

13006

VOLUME 2

THE BOOK OF

GENESIS

Charles T. Fritsch

JOHN KNOX PRESS
RICHMOND, VIRGINIA

© C. D. Deans 1959

Published in Great Britain by SCM Press Ltd., London. Published simultaneously in Canada by The Ryerson Press, Toronto.

Sixth printing 1970

International Standard Book Number: 0-8042-3002-X
Library of Congress Catalog Card Number: 59-10454
Printed in the United States of America

PREFACE

The LAYMAN'S BIBLE COMMENTARY is based on the conviction that the Bible has the Word of good news for the whole world. The Bible is not the property of a special group. It is not even the property and concern of the Church alone. It is given to the Church for its own life but also to bring God's offer of life to all mankind —wherever there are ears to hear and hearts to respond.

It is this point of view which binds the separate parts of the LAYMAN'S BIBLE COMMENTARY into a unity. There are many volumes and many writers, coming from varied backgrounds, as is the case with the Bible itself. But also as with the Bible there is a unity of purpose and of faith. The purpose is to clarify the situations and language of the Bible that it may be more and more fully understood. The faith is that in the Bible there is essentially one Word, one message of salvation, one gospel.

The LAYMAN'S BIBLE COMMENTARY is designed to be a concise non-technical guide for the layman in personal study of his own Bible. Therefore, no biblical text is printed along with the comment upon it. This commentary will have done its work precisely to the degree in which it moves its readers to take up the Bible for themselves.

The writers have used the Revised Standard Version of the Bible as their basic text. Occasionally they have differed from this translation. Where this is the case they have given their reasons. In the main, no attempt has been made either to justify the wording of the Revised Standard Version or to compare it with other translations.

The objective in this commentary is to provide the most helpful explanation of fundamental matters in simple, up-to-date terms. Exhaustive treatment of subjects has not been undertaken.

In our age knowledge of the Bible is perilously low. At the same time there are signs that many people are longing for help in getting such knowledge. Knowledge of and about the Bible is, of course, not enough. The grace of God and the work of the Holy Spirit are essential to the renewal of life through the Scriptures. It is in the happy confidence that the great hunger for the Word is a sign of God's grace already operating within men, and that the Spirit works most wonderfully where the Word is familiarly known, that this commentary has been written and published.

THE EDITORS AND
THE PUBLISHERS

THE BOOK OF

GENESIS

___

INTRODUCTION

The Purpose of the Book of Genesis

The Book of Genesis is the book of beginnings. It tells about
"the generations of the heavens and the earth when they were created" (2:4a). (It is from the Greek translation of the Hebrew
word for "generations" in this verse that the name "Genesis" is
derived.) It tells about the beginning of life and the creation of
man. It describes the beginnings of family life with the marriage of
the first man and woman and the birth of their children. The entrance of sin into the world, with its dire consequences for all mankind, is skillfully and graphically portrayed. The Book of Genesis
preserves ancient traditions about the beginnings of urban and
nomadic cultures and the various arts associated with primitive
society. Finally, with the call of Abraham, it describes the beginning of the carrying out of God's redemptive purpose in history
whereby mankind is to be saved through a people specially chosen.

Some of the stories in the early chapters of Genesis were *originally* aetiological in character; that is, they tried to explain some of
the persistent and common questions of life. For instance, the creation of Eve out of Adam's rib explains the strong sexual attraction
of man and woman. The divine curse upon the serpent, the woman,
and the man explains mankind's inherent hatred of snakes, the
suffering of childbirth, and the fact that man has to work so hard
to eke out his livelihood from the hostile soil. The Cain and Abel
story probably reflects the ancient feuding that went on between the
agricultural and nomadic ways of life. The Tower of Babel story
explains how the differences arose among the languages of the
world. Then, too, some of the stories were mainly etymological in
character, explaining the significance of the names of individuals
(for example, Noah, 5:29; Isaac, 21:6; Jacob, 25:26) or of cultic
sites (for example, Beer-sheba, 21:25-32; Bethel, 28:18-22; Penuel, 32:30-32). But when these stories became a part of the Gen-

esis narrative, they lost their purely "explanation" character, and took on deeper theological significance in the context of Israel's faith.

The main purpose of the Book of Genesis, however, is to show that the God of Israel is the God of *creation* as well as the God of the *Covenant*. The God who created the universe is the God who called Abraham in order that through him all the families of the earth might be blessed (12:3, margin). The God who created the world is the God who made a covenant with Abraham and his seed in order that through them God's redemptive purpose might be made known to all mankind (17:7). At a later time in Israel's history a prophet of the Exile explicitly states that "God, the LORD, who created the heavens and stretched them out," and "spread forth the earth and what comes from it," called his servant Israel before birth to be the Covenant people for the salvation of the world (see Isa. 42:5-6; 49:5-6; also 43:15 where God is called "the Creator of Israel"). By setting the patriarchal history (Gen. 12-50) in the framework of creation and universal history (Gen. 1-11), the writer of the Book of Genesis is teaching us not only that the goal of creation is the Covenant, but that the ultimate goal of the Covenant is the salvation of the whole world (12:3). It was through Israel's faith in the Covenant God who had chosen her and delivered her from Egypt and directed her steps through history that Israel came to know more fully the Creator God.

Authorship and Date of the Book of Genesis

Before discussing the problem of the authorship and date of the Book of Genesis in detail, there are one or two matters of general importance which should be considered. First of all, it should be remembered that Genesis was not always a separate book of the Bible. It originally formed a part of the Jewish Torah, or Law, which, for the sake of convenience, was divided into five books, often called the "Pentateuch" (a Greek word meaning "five volumes"). Although the Book of Genesis forms a natural unit or division by itself, it is closely related to the account of the Exodus which follows it, for the deliverance from Egypt and the entrance into the Promised Land were regarded as the fulfillment of the promise given to Abraham (see 17:4-7), and renewed with Isaac (26:24) and Jacob (28:13-15; also 50:24). Since, therefore, what we know as the Book of Genesis was an integral part of the whole Pentateuch, much that we shall say about the way it was written will apply to the whole work.

It should be remembered, too, that in ancient times authorship of a book meant something quite different from what it means today with our strict copyright laws and the long legal contracts between publisher and author. Most of the apocalyptic writings, which flourished after 200 B.C., appeared under assumed names. In the Old Testament itself much of the Wisdom Literature, written over a period of a thousand years, was attributed to Solomon, the patron saint of the wise men and writer of many proverbs (see I Kings 4:29-34). The Book of Proverbs, for instance, is entitled "The proverbs of Solomon, son of David, king of Israel" (Prov. 1:1), even though, by its own statement, it includes collections of wise sayings written by other men (see Prov. 30:1; 31:1). Compare also "The Song of Songs, which is Solomon's" (Song of Solomon 1:1) and the Wisdom of Solomon and the Psalms of Solomon from the Intertestament period. It is evident that wise men from a later time felt that they were actually writing in the spirit of Solomon, the ideal wise man of Israel, so they ascribed their works to him. Another example is found in the fact that many of the hymns of Israel, composed over a long period of time, were added to the basic collection of psalms ascribed to David, the great hymn writer of Israel.

It was in the same general way that Moses' name became attached to the legal lore of Israel. Moses was the founder of the theocratic state of Israel and the first to formulate the laws which were to determine the character and life of Israel for all time to come (see Exod. 24:4). Since all later codifications of law in Israel were actually expansions and modifications of the basic laws of Moses, the tradition of Mosaic authorship became attached to the whole body of laws found in the Pentateuch. Therefore in Jewish tradition Moses became known as the author of the Pentateuch, even though it is nowhere stated in the books themselves that he wrote them.

On the contrary, in Genesis, which is our main concern here, there are clear indications that the book, as we have it, was written long after the days of Moses. There are chronological notations and historical references which can only be interpreted to mean that the stories found in Genesis were written down long after the events which they describe had taken place. For instance, in 22:14 and 26:33 certain Canaanite place names, associated with patriarchal history, are given in forms more familiar to the Israelites of a later day, and in 35:20 it is stated that "the pillar of Rachel's tomb" exists "to this day"; that is, to the time when Israel is in the land. The phrase, "at that time the Canaanites were in the land" (12:6; see 13:7), is obviously an historical aside, by which the writer means to compare the days of the patriarchs, when the Canaanites were in possession of the land, with his own time when the Israelites had conquered the land for themselves. The reference to the Philistines in 21:32 and 26:1 as the inhabitants of southwestern Palestine during the days of Abraham and Isaac appears to be chronologically out of place since we know from archaeological evidence, as well as from the implication of biblical history itself, that these people did not settle in Palestine until after 1200 B.C. Also the expression, "before any king reigned over the Israelites" (36:31), implies that the writer was acquainted with the monarchy as a recognized form of government in Israel, although the monarchy came centuries after the events described in Genesis. These and other expressions of a similar nature, found throughout the Pentateuch, seem to indicate that these books were written when the Israelites were in possession of the land of Canaan.

Then, too, a careful study of the text of Genesis indicates that the book is a compilation of several different literary sources, written over a long period of time. One does not have to read very far into Genesis before noticing that some of the stories are recorded in two or more different versions. For instance, there are two different accounts of creation, in 1:1—2:4a and 2:4b-25. There are two different traditions regarding the number of animals that went into the ark (6:19-20 and 7:2-3). The promise of a son to Sarah is recorded two times (17:16-19 and 18:10-15). Jacob is blessed twice by Isaac (27:27-29 and 28:1-4). There are several accounts of the naming of Beer-sheba (21:31 and 26:33), Bethel (28:18-19 and 35:14-15; compare 12:8 and 13:3), and Israel (32:28 and 35:10); and the association of the name Isaac with the idea of laughter is noted three times (17:17; 18:12-15; and 21:6).

A careful reader will also notice a number of minor discrepancies in the stories of Genesis. Abraham, for instance, laughs at the idea of having a son when he is a hundred years old (17:17), yet, according to 25:1-6, after the death of Sarah he takes another wife, Keturah, and has children by her. Isaac is about one hundred years old and at the point of death when Jacob flees from Esau (27:41), yet, according to 35:28, Isaac lives to be one hundred and eighty years of age. Other examples could be added.

It is believed by most students today that these difficulties and discrepancies can best be explained by assuming that the Book of Genesis is composed of several literary sources, written at different times and containing similar, but not identical, accounts of the same stories. In the course of more than two centuries of intensive, critical study of the texts, students have come to discern three major literary strands which were woven together to form the Book of Genesis as we have it today. These may be distinguished from one another by their *use of the names for God,* by *characteristics of language and style,* and by their *distinct theological points of view.* A brief description of each of these sources follows.

J. This symbol designates the literary strand in which a Hebrew word, rendered by Lord in the Revised Standard Version (Jehovah —Jahweh in German—or Yahweh) is used almost exclusively as the name for God. The "J document," which includes the bulk of material in Genesis (see Outline), was probably written during the period of the United Kingdom, about 950 B.C. The gifted writers, or writer, of this document—it could have been composed by a group of theologians or by one person—gathered together the ancient traditions of Israel and wrote them down to form a literary masterpiece which reflects Israel's faith in God and in his overruling redemptive purpose in the history of his people. This author, or authors, designated the Yahwist, sees in the Exodus experience and the conquest of Canaan which are described in the Books of Exodus through Joshua, the fulfillment of the promise given to Abraham (Gen. 12:1-3). This promise, in turn, is linked with the ultimate salvation of the whole world, whose tragic history is recounted in Genesis 1-11. In writing this grandly conceived epic of Israel's history the Yahwist reveals his own deep faith in God, whom he is fond of describing in anthropomorphic language; that is, in terms descriptive of man's physical or emotional life. He is interested in the origins of the names of places and persons, and his character delineations are unsurpassed in the Old Testament.

E. This symbol denotes the literary strand in which the Hebrew names "Elohim" and "El" for God predominate. For many reasons it is believed that this "E document" was written in the Northern Kingdom of Israel around 850 to 750 B.C. The material ascribed to it in Genesis is far less in extent than that which is ascribed to J. Passages which describe the Deity as appearing to people in visions (15:1-2), in dreams (20:1-17; 28:10-12; 31:10, 24), or in the form of an angel (21:17; 22:11; 31:11; 32:1), are characteristic of E. The writer of this document does not normally show the power and skill of expression that appears in J, yet one of the most striking passages in Genesis—the sacrifice of Isaac (22:1-13)—comes from the pen of E.

P. This symbol denotes the literary strand which is ascribed to priestly sources, or to one of the priests who compiled and wrote down these sources sometime after the Exile. In Genesis this material consists mainly of the account of creation found in 1:1—2:4a, elements of the story of the Flood (6-8), genealogies (5, 10, and other lists scattered throughout the book), the Covenant chapters (9, 17), the story of the purchase of the cave of Machpelah (23), the blessing of Jacob by Isaac (27:46—28:9), and the numerous references to dates and to the vital statistics of the patriarchs which appear throughout the book. The rather mechanical framework of the Book of Genesis is attributed to this writer. He divides the history of the patriarchal period into ten main sections, each beginning with the phrase, "these are the generations of" (see 2:4a, where the phrase concludes the section dealing with creation; 5:1; 6:9; 10:1; 11:10, 27; 25:12, 19; 36:1, [9]; 37:2). P is systematic and orderly in the presentation of his material, but his repetitious use of stereotyped phrases and formulae makes his work seem stilted and pedantic. Yet some of the deepest theological insights into the nature of God and the world found anywhere in Scripture have been preserved in the priestly teaching on creation (1:1—2:4a) and the Covenant (9 and 17).

Even though these various literary sources of Genesis were written approximately between 950 and 550 B.C., they all contain very ancient material which has been expanded and reinterpreted according to the theological viewpoint of each writer. Chapter 14 does not seem to belong to any of these literary documents, and the Joseph story was probably a literary unit written down long before it got into the hands of the writers of these documents. The Book of Genesis took shape as these strands were gradually woven together. First, the two independent but parallel narratives, J and E, were combined to form the "JE document." This took place shortly after the fall of the Northern Kingdom (721 B.C.). Then, sometime after the fall of the Southern Kingdom (587 B.C.), the JE epic was joined to P, which served as the framework for the story. In this way the Book of Genesis, as we know it, was born.

The Message of the Book of Genesis

The Book of Genesis is the starting point of all theology. Its teachings about God and man, the nature of sin, and the divine plan of redemption are fundamental to the understanding of both the Old and New Testaments. Fortunately for us the writer, in true oriental fashion, has clothed his discussion of some of the most profound theological problems in language of such simplicity and symbolic imagery that even a child can understand it. It is only when we realize that the oriental mind thinks in pictures and expresses itself in nonphilosophical, poetic language that we can truly appreciate the stories of Genesis 1-11 and interpret them correctly. If, for instance, we try to apply our scientific ways of thinking to the account of creation in Genesis 1 and 2, or if we try to literalize a talking serpent, we are obscuring the message of these stories. In reading the opening chapters of Genesis we must put ourselves in the place of the writer; we must try to understand his point of view and modes of expression if we want to know what he really means. In a word, if we want to unlock the spiritual treasures of the Bible, we must enter into the mood in which it was written and interpret it on its own terms.

The rest of the Book of Genesis (12-50) is given over to the life stories of four characters—Abraham, Isaac, Jacob, and Joseph. In these narratives we learn how God called and trained the patriarchs to become worthy recipients of the divine promise, that through them all the nations might be blessed. Abraham's trust and obedience in the face of severe testings make him the example of faith for both the Jew and the Christian. In the story of Jacob we see how God can change a stubborn, scheming man into a vessel fit for the divine blessing. Joseph's phenomenal success in the court of a foreign ruler is attributed to his strength of character in the face of temptation and his faith in the overruling providence of God. In the wanderings of the patriarchs and in their victories and defeats, the man of faith sees the pilgrimage of his own soul as he makes his way slowly and arduously toward the City of God.

From the record of God's activity with his people in Genesis we learn a great deal about the nature of God, man, sin, and redemption which is presupposed in the rest of the Scriptures. It is important, therefore, to consider in some detail these basic theological truths which undergird the faith of Israel and the Church.

God

God is the Sovereign Lord of creation. By his mighty Word the world is created, order is brought out of chaos, light conquers darkness, and the wild and fearful sea is brought under control. All created things in their appointed places bow in praise and adoration before the Lord their Maker. The God of Abraham, Isaac, and Jacob is the one and only God of heaven, whose rule and power extend beyond the boundaries of Canaan. He cares for the patriarchs in foreign lands; he is honored by Hittite (23:6), "Philistine" (26:28), and Egyptian (41:39) alike; and he even appears to Laban, the Aramean, and Abimelech, the "Philistine," in dreams. His presence goes with the patriarchs in their wanderings, and men call upon his name in worship without priest or temple. The mercy of God extends beyond his elect, for he protects the vagabond Cain with a sign; he has a blessing for Ishmael and Esau after they are rejected; and, above all, he chooses Abraham so that through him and his seed the nations of the world may be blessed. It is remarkable that this view of God as having blessing for all is shared by the three main sources—J, E, and P—of Genesis.

Man

Man is created in the image of God to think his thoughts after him and enjoy him forever. As the crown of God's creation and as the representative of God on earth, man has dominion over the realm of nature. This sovereignty he holds as a trust from God. He is master of the world only as long as he recognizes his dependence upon God, the Creator of the world. When, however, man tries to become like God and usurp powers which belong to God alone, he loses his regal position and lives in fear of God and the world of nature. Because of his superior technical knowledge, man today seems to be the ruler of the created order, but the fears of self-destruction which continually beset him reveal the weakness and insecurity of his position apart from God. In Jesus Christ, the last Adam (I Cor. 15:45), we see what we might have been had not sin entered the world. In him we can become what God intended us to be (Heb. 2:8-9).

Sin

The essence of sin is rebellion against God, arising from man's exalted opinion of himself and his desire to be like God. This spirit of rebellion is expressed basically in disobedience to God's word and multiplies in any number of sinful acts. The primary theme of Genesis 1-11 is sin and judgment, with sporadic rays of hope breaking through. In the story of the Fall, sin is depicted as disobedience to God's word; in the Cain and Abel episode it is wanton violence; in the Flood story it is moral depravity; and in the account of the Tower of Babel it is pride. In each of these cases God judges the sinner, but in each case God tempers his judgment with mercy. God pronounces the curse of death upon Adam, but he mercifully allows him to live out his normal span of life. God condemns Cain to a life of endless wandering, but he mercifully puts a mark upon him, so that when strangers see him they will not slay him. God condemns the human race to complete annihilation by a flood, but he mercifully perpetuates mankind by saving one man and his family. God scatters the proud of the earth as they try to reach the sky with their tower, but he mercifully makes provision for their salvation by calling Abraham (12:3).

Even the people specially chosen by God are not represented in Genesis as immune to sin. Israel could always look at herself and her history realistically. Because of her faith in the goodness of God and in his ultimate victory over sin, Israel never became morbidly introspective.

One of the best expressions of the true nature of sin in the Old Testament is found in Joseph's words to Potiphar's wicked wife: "How then can I do this great wickedness, and sin against God?" (39:9). With true prophetic insight Joseph sees that sin is basically an act of defiance against God (see Ps. 51:4), and that any sin committed against one's fellow man is a sin against God.

Redemption

The dramatic story of redemption begins with the entrance of sin into the world. As soon as man falls prey to the wiles of the Evil One, God is on hand searching for him in the garden (3:8-9). No truer picture of the Savior God can be found anywhere in Scripture. The God who is revealed to us in the Bible is a personal God who created man in his own image to have fellowship with him. When that fellowship is broken by sin, God immediately takes steps to restore it. It is God who initiates the drama of redemption because he loves man and wants him for himself. God condescends to tread the earth in search of man who has rebelled against him. God offers man the opportunity to repent, and his act of clothing man is an expression of his grace as he covers the shame and guilt of man so that he can face his Maker again. Salvation is solely from God, from beginning to end.

We have seen how God's mercy accompanies his judgment upon sin. Man's sin is always a challenge to God's love, but love always prevails. In the Book of Genesis, God's love for the world is supremely manifested in the election of Abraham to be the channel of God's blessings to all the families of the earth (12:3). Once again God takes the initiative in the drama of redemption, for "the LORD" is the subject of the first sentence of holy history (12:1). We should never forget that God is the main character of the Book of Genesis, as well as of the whole Bible. He manifests his presence in history to bring salvation to mankind when he binds himself to Abraham and to his seed in an everlasting Covenant (17:7). In this way, God mercifully assures mankind that he will be faithful to the promise he made to Abraham that through him and his seed all the nations of the world are to be blessed. After Abraham dies, God renews his Covenant pledge with Isaac (26:24) and with Jacob (28:13-14), and raises up Joseph to save his people in the days of famine. The blessings of the Covenant are assured for future generations by Joseph's last words and act (50:24-25).

OUTLINE

COMMENTARY

PRIMEVAL HISTORY

Genesis 1—11

Creation (1:1—2:25)

Creation, according to the biblical account, is the free, spontaneous act of a wise and sovereign God. He commands, and the world comes into being; he speaks, and all things are created by his word. The wisdom of the Creator is reflected in the orderliness of the cosmos; his goodness is woven into the very texture of the universe. Yet creation is not God; the forces of nature are never deified in the religion of Israel. In course of time Israel comes to see that the Creator God is the Covenant God, who freely elects Abraham and his seed to be a blessing to the world (Gen. 12:1-3), and creates Israel to be his servant (Isa. 42:5-6; 49:5). And the God who creates the heavens and the earth in the beginning will re-create creation at the end so that heaven and earth, which were rent by sin, will be united once again (see Isa. 65:17; Rev. 21: 1-4). Only in him can there be a true beginning and a true end, for he is the Alpha and the Omega, the first and the last, the beginning and the end (Rev. 22:13).

The Two Accounts of Creation [P, J]

The Book of Genesis opens with two accounts of creation which differ in language, style, theological point of view, and the order of events in the creation. The first story, found in Genesis 1:1—2:4a, is a finely wrought literary document in which the creative activity of God is spelled out in orderly progression with carefully chosen words and recurring stereotyped expressions. The writer is obviously a priestly theologian (P) who views the universe as God's temple in which all created things, arranged liturgically in classes, are worshiping their Maker. The Sabbath is sanctioned by the Deity as a day of rest from the very beginning, and the calendar of sacred feasts is regulated by the heavenly clock which is composed of the sun, moon, and stars. Over this cosmic congregation man, the crown of God's creation, presides as the divinely appointed high priest. The whole chapter may be regarded as a creation hymn in which all nature joins in praising the divine Creator.

The second story of creation, found in Genesis 2:4b-25, is quite different from the first. It is much more vivid and exuberant than the first account, and the style is more simple. The writer (usually designated J because he prefers the Hebrew name for God which is translated "LORD" in the Revised Standard Version) is less skillful than P in weaving his sources together, and far less interested in matters pertaining to worship and ritual. His conception of God is more anthropomorphic than P's; that is, he thinks of God in human terms, ascribing to him human actions like *molding* clay, *breathing, planting,* and *building.*

The difference in structure between these two accounts may best be shown by outlining their contents in parallel columns:

P	J
The creative acts are compressed into a schematic pattern of six days:	No schematic pattern of time:
1. Light	1. Man
2. Firmament	2. Garden in Eden
3. Dry land; Vegetation	3. Trees, including the Tree of Life, and the Tree of the Knowledge of Good and Evil
4. Luminaries	
5. Birds; Fish	
6. Animals; Man (kind)	4. Animals
	5. Woman

The significance of these differences will be discussed later.

Even though there are obvious differences between the two Hebrew traditions of creation, the basic theological ideas underlying them are the same. In both accounts the one true and living God is the sovereign Lord of creation. He is prior to, and distinct from, the finite, material universe which he creates. Both stories teach that man is the crown of God's creation and that God has given him dominion over the animals. By placing man last in the order of creation, and by arranging the creative acts as he does—vegetation, birds, fish, beasts, and then man—P is showing the pre-eminence of man over all created things. At the same time J, by placing man at the first of the creation story and making the trees, the animals, and woman subservient to his needs, is saying the same thing about man as P, only in a different way.

It is most fitting that the story of creation, with its profound theological insights into the nature of God, man, and the universe, should be found on the opening pages of the Bible, for it is fundamental to the theology of both the Old and the New Testaments.

The First Account of Creation (1:1—2:4a) [P]

Genesis opens with one of the most sublime verses in Scripture. It is a brief, simple, yet remarkably profound statement of the divine act of creation which is spelled out in the rest of the chapter. It is as if with one stroke of the pen the inspired author has cleared the sky of heathen gods and the human mind of false theories regarding the beginning of things. In place of the fighting, jealous gods who appear in the ancient story of creation circulating in Babylonia, we find here the one, true, personal, and living God, whose existence is unquestioned and whose authority is unchallenged. He stands transcendent and sovereign at the beginning, before the world, as we know it, was created, an idea which is further developed in John 1:1 and I John 1:1. He is the powerful One, as Elohim, the Hebrew name for God throughout this chapter, indicates. His supreme wisdom is manifest in the orderliness of the cosmos, or "the heavens and the earth," as the Hebrews called it, and his infinite goodness is woven into the structure of the universe where all things fulfill his purpose (vss. 4, 10, 12, 18, 21, 25, 31).

The doctrine of creation which this verse teaches is in direct opposition to many of the man-made philosophies about the origin and nature of the world. The statement that "God created the heavens and the earth" denies, for instance, the view that matter is eternal and the whole of reality, and the view that the universe came about by a purely mechanistic process. It also shows that God is separate from his creation, and so cannot be identified with nature in any way.

The Hebrew word translated "create" in verses 1, 21, and 27 of this chapter, is a theological term used exclusively in the Old Testament of divine creative activity. In Isaiah 40-66, where its theological significance is most clearly expressed, it is used about twenty times. There God is the creator of the universe (Isa. 42:5; 45:7-9), of Israel (Isa. 43:1, 15), and of the new heavens and earth in the Golden Age (Isa. 65:17); and it is the creative power of God which ensures the success of the Servant's mission (Isa. 42:5-9; 49:5-6). The writer of Psalm 51, who confesses his heinous sin before God, realizes that only the divine power that created the universe can make a new "creation" out of him (Ps. 51:10, where the verb "to create" is used; see also II Cor. 5:17). Although the idea of the Creator-God was known to Israel in pre-exilic times

(Gen. 2:4b-9; Deut. 4:32; Amos 4:13), it was not until postexilic times that the full significance of this doctrine was realized.

Associated with this theological term are the ideas that God's creative activity is free and unnecessitated, and that what God creates is totally new and marvelous (see Exod. 34:10). God is the sovereign, transcendent Lord of creation, who brings the cosmos into being by his word and will (Ps. 33:6-9; Jer. 10:12).

Whether the writer of Genesis 1:1 meant creation out of nothing, his use of the word for "create" does not make certain. Etymologically the word seems to come from a root meaning "to form by cutting" or "to build." In any case, when the word is used in the Old Testament with the meaning "create," God is its exclusive subject. This, plus the fact that it is never used with an object out of which something is fashioned, would seem to indicate that it could have meant "creation out of nothing." It was not until a later time, however, that this idea was explicitly stated (as in the Apocryphal work II Macc. 7:28; compare Heb. 11:3).

With the support of the ancient versions and as the English translation indicates, we take verse 1 as a complete, independent sentence, a preface to the story of creation which follows. In sharp contrast with the orderly heavens and earth, the *cosmos* of verse 1, created by the will of a free and sovereign God, is the formless void, the *chaos* of verse 2, over which the divine Spirit broods like a mighty bird to effect the miracle of creation (see also Deut. 32:11). Here the underlying conception of creation is a struggle between the Deity and certain forces of nature in which the mysterious, invisible divine power brings order out of chaos, conquers the realm of darkness, and subdues the wild and boundless sea.

The recital of the creative acts of God now proceeds in rapid tempo. The repeated phrase, "and God said" (vss. 3, 6, 9, 11, 14, 20, 24, 26, 28, 29), indicates that God creates by his word (as in Ps. 33:6-9). Creation is the product of God's personal will, of which his word is the outward expression. God's word not only creates nature, but history as well (I Kings 2:27; 8:24). Creation by the divine word denotes the unconditional sovereignty and power of God. He speaks, and the world is created (see Isa. 55:11). By speaking this creative word God shows that he is a personal God, and the nature of the word is such that it shows that he expects a response from that which he creates. This concept of the word which God spoke at creation, without which nothing was made that was made, was in the mind of the New Testament

writers as they spoke of the Word which became flesh and taber-
nacled among us, full of grace and truth (John 1:3-14; see also
Col. 1:16; Heb. 1:2).

Light is the first created thing, the indispensable condition of
all life and growth on earth. It is evidently conceived of here as
independent of the heavenly luminaries, since they do not appear
until verse 16. It is tempting to think of this light as the glory of
God, the light of God's own presence (Ps. 104:2; Rev. 21:23),
but the Hebrew expression, "and the light came into existence,"
indicates that light is a distinct creation, and not an emanation
from God. In the creation of light God shows that he is the con-
queror of the darkness which enveloped the "deep" (vs. 2), a victory which is dramatically re-enacted with the dawn of each new
day. Having divided the light from the darkness God assigns to
each of these elements its own abode (see also Job 38:19).

The phrase, "and there was evening and there was morning,"
found at the close of each of the six days of creation, reveals
the Jewish custom of reckoning a day from sunset to sunset.
That the writer had in mind literal days in this chapter is made
clear by the hallowing of the seventh day in 2:2-3. Therefore, to
interpret "day" in these passages as a long period of a thousand
years (as in Ps. 90:4; II Peter 3:8), or a geological period, is
both unnecessary and incorrect.

On the second day (1:6-8) God makes the firmament, which
the ancients thought of as a solid, bowl-like structure overarch-
ing the earth (see Ps. 104:5; Job 26:11). To this vault of heaven,
separating the upper waters from the waters below, are attached
the luminaries which rule the day and night. Rain is caused by
opening the sluice gates of heaven (Ps. 78:23). The rivers and
seas and springs on earth are fed by the subterranean waters.

On the third day (1:9-13) two creative acts take place—the
separation of the dry land from the waters which were under
the heavens, and the production of vegetation. Psalm 104:6-8
gives an excellent description of the appearance of the earth
after the waters recede. That God could set a bound for the
waters of the deep to keep them in place was always a source of
amazement to the Hebrews (Job 38:8-11; Ps. 104:9; Jer. 5:22).

After the dry land is firmly established amid the seas (see Ps.
24:2), it is clothed, by divine command, with verdant vegetation
consisting of two kinds of plant life: the herbs, which produce
seeds in themselves, and the trees which produce seed-bearing

fruit. The author takes special care to note that the various species of plant and animal life (vss. 12, 21, and 24) are determined by divine command from the very beginning. This emphasis upon divinely imposed distinctions in nature reflects the concern of the priesthood to distinguish between clean and unclean animals, between man and animal (Lev. 18:23), and even between man and woman (see Deut. 22:5). God is not a God of confusion, but of order (see Isa. 45:18; I Cor. 14:33), and all creation reflects the orderliness of its Maker.

On the fourth day (1:14-19) the luminaries, or bodies of light, come into existence. Their purpose is threefold. First, they are "to separate the day from the night." Even though light has already been divided from darkness, and the alternation of evening and morning has been referred to several times, the writer does not mention the making of the luminaries to rule over the day and night until this point in the scheme of creation. By their presence in the firmament the distinction between day and night apparently becomes more pronounced.

Secondly, the luminaries are to serve as a cosmic clock, designating the calendar days and years, and regulating the appointed seasons with their liturgical feasts. The world view underlying this verse is obviously geocentric, which means that the earth is the center of the universe and that all the heavenly bodies were made to serve it. In the light of modern astronomical discoveries this theory, of course, is no longer tenable. The purpose of Genesis, moreover, is not to give scientific theories, ancient or modern. Yet from the religious point of view there is much to be said for the description of the universe given in these verses. Wonderful and impressive as the heavenly bodies are, there is no hint in the Genesis story that they were to be worshiped, as they were in the pagan religions of the Near East. Rather are they created to glorify God (see Ps. 19:1) and to subserve the needs of man, who is far greater than all the phenomena of nature (see Ps. 8:3-5). In particular their religious function is to indicate the rhythm of the festal seasons—the new moon, the full moon, the recurring festivals of seedtime and harvest—and thus they ever remind man that God is the Lord of time.

Thirdly, God has set the luminaries in their courses "to give light upon the earth." Here again they are described in their relation to earth, especially as they benefit all living organisms by day and as they guide the wayfarer on land or sea by night.

Just as the light of the first day corresponds with the "lights" of the fourth day, so the appearance of the firmament and the division of the waters on the second day prepare the way for the creation of the fowl and aquatic animals on the fifth day (1:20-23). For the second time "create" is used (1:21; compare vs. 1). In this context the word emphasizes the fact that the principle of life, common to man and the other creatures (see 1:27), is derived from God alone. The divine blessing, expressed in the words "be fruitful and multiply," gives to creatures (and man, 1:28) the special power of self-propagation. The variety and multiplicity of animate life attest to the mighty power released by this blessing. The continuing power of the divine creative energy is seen in the preservation and propagation of life (see Neh. 9:6, where the expression, "thou preservest all of them" is literally "thou [art] keeping all of them alive").

The parallelism of the first and second days of creation with the fourth and fifth days is continued in the correspondence between the appearance of the land masses, clothed with verdant plant life, on the third day and the creation of the land animals, including man, and the provision of vegetation for their food, on the sixth day (1:24-31). The creation of man is pictured (1:26) as the result of God's deliberation with his heavenly court (see also I Kings 22:19-22; Isa. 6:1; etc.). There is no word of command as in other places in the chapter, simply a word of reflection. That the word "man" or *adam* is used here in the generic sense of "mankind" is shown by verse 27, in which the word *adam* is parallel with "male and female." Mankind is created in the image of God.

What the phrase, "in our image, after our likeness" (1:26), signifies is difficult to determine. Generally it is taken to mean that man receives from God a divine stamp which differentiates him from the animals. Although man has much in common with the animals, he is far superior to them because of his special relation to his Maker, and he is given dominion over them (1:28). More specifically we can say that man is made for fellowship with God. He can think God's thoughts after him, and enjoy him forever. But the Hebrew word for "image" means more than spiritual resemblance or self-conscious reason. Literally it means "something that is cut out," as, for example, the "image" of a heathen god (see II Kings 11:18; Amos 5:26; Ezek. 7:20), and so it suggests something concrete and substantial in form and appearance. This basic meaning of the word cannot be ignored in this passage. Throughout the history of Israel, God's form was seen by men in visions and appearances of various kinds. It was that form which God stamped upon man at the creation. The substantial nature of this image is further confirmed by Genesis 5:3, which states that "he [Adam] became the father of a son in his own likeness, after his *image*," which can only mean that the image received by Adam from God at creation is passed on from one generation to another (see also Gen. 9:6). Perhaps the writer wished to offset the materialistic conception of the word "image" in 1:26 by adding the qualifying phrase, "after our likeness" (or, resemblance). The image of God in man, which was marred by sin, is revealed in perfect clarity in the Incarnation, in the person of Jesus Christ. The very fact that man was created in the divine image shows the possibility of God's becoming flesh and dwelling among us.

The third occurrence of the theological term "to create" is found in verse 27, where it is used of the creation of man. God's special creative power, expressed by this word, is the only explanation we have for the origin of matter (vs. 1), sentient life (1:21), and man as a distinct creation (1:27).

The tenth divine utterance, "and God said" (1:29), makes provision for food for man and beast. Before the Fall, both man and animals subsisted purely on a vegetable diet. Since God provided the food for his creatures, there would have been no bloodshed or struggle for existence in his creation (see also Matt. 6:25-33). "Peace on earth" was God's goal from the beginning, as the idyllic description of the Garden of Eden reveals (ch. 2).

God's stamp of approval upon his creation is expressed in the words, "Behold, it was very good." The work of each day was "good," but now as God contemplates the whole of creation, he declares it to be "very good." According to Hebrew psychology, matter is not inherently evil and nature is not hostile to God. All things are created in their order to perform their special functions. The universe and all its "host" (2:1) are ready to offer their praise and worship to their Creator on the Sabbath day.

After completing the work of creation, God set apart the seventh day for rest (2:1-4a). He "blessed" it, by which it was given special life-giving powers, and he "hallowed" it, to be set apart for holy uses. A Sabbath without honoring God is a lie. In this passage the divine sanction of the Sabbath goes back to the creation of the world when God rested on the seventh day (see Exod. 20:11; 31:17; see also Deut. 5:15, which gives another view of the significance of the Sabbath). The Sabbath rest, initiated and ordained by God, was shattered by sin. Never fully restored in the Old Testament (Ps. 95:11), the true Sabbath rest remains for those who have fellowship with God in Christ (Heb. 3:7—4:10). The earthly Sabbath is a foretaste of that unbroken fellowship which the true believer will have with God in eternity.

The word "generations" (2:4a) is used in the priestly document of Genesis as an introductory formula for the ten sections of the patriarchal history (5:1; 6:9; 10:1; 11:10, 27; 25:12, 19; 36:1, [9]; 37:2). In 2:4a it comes at the end of the story of creation, and should probably be translated literally, "begettings, or births," of the heavens and the earth, "when they were created" by God. Just as in the birth of a human being a new person comes out of the unknown to take its place, where nothing had been before, so the writer here is thinking of the creation of the universe as a birth brought about by the divine creative power.

The Second Account of Creation (2:4b-25) [J]

"In the day that the LORD God made the earth and the heavens" is the way that J introduces his account of creation (2:4b). The differences between this statement and the first verse of Genesis indicate that we are dealing with two separate accounts of the creation. (See the Introduction for a discussion of this problem.) "In the day," if taken literally, means that creation did not take place in six days, as in the first chapter; but this phrase may also mean simply "when," as commonly used in the Old Testament (see Jer. 11:4). The designation of the Deity by the combined names, Lord God, is rarely found outside of the early chapters of Genesis. "LORD" is printed in large and small capital letters in the Revised Standard Version to indicate that it represents the Hebrew YHWH, the name of God revealed to Moses when he was called (Exod. 3:14). According to Genesis 4:26, however, the name was known as far back as the time of Seth. The unusual order of the words, "the earth and the heavens," may be due to the fact that J, in his account of creation, is concerned mainly with this earth and with man who was placed here by God as his creature. Many of the cosmic aspects of P's account in Genesis 1 are missing in J. Finally, the more prosaic word "make" is used in the J account rather than the theological term for "create" found in P.

After the introductory statement of 2:4b, the writer describes the earth as originally waterless and plantless, obviously corresponding to conditions described by the phrase "without form and void" in 1:2. We are also told that there was no man to till the ground. From under the earth the subterranean waters (see marginal reading "flood," which is better than "mist" in 2:6) break through and moisten the ground. In this account the waters are a source of blessing, rather than an enemy of God as they seem to be in 1:2. Obviously the background of J's story of creation is a dry, barren wasteland which is able to produce vegetation only after a heavy rainfall. With the coming of water, one expects to read about the growth of plant life, but this is by-passed so that man may be brought upon the scene as soon as possible. The ground is prepared so that God can form man out of the clay (2:7). In the Hebrew the two words translated "ground" and "man" are very much alike. The verb "to form," found in this verse, is the technical word used of the potter forming the clay into a vessel (see Jer. 18:1-11). That God uses clay to form man shows that man and the ground go together. Man is of the earth, earthy (I Cor. 15:47). There is no reason for false pride in man. He can never become equal to God. After God had formed man out of clay, he "breathed into his nostrils the breath of life; and man became a living being." It is important to note that in 2:19, when God forms the animals and the fowl of the air, the writer does not say that God breathes into them the breath of life. This indicates that there is a distinct difference between man and animal. Man receives life as a gift from God. This is what is meant by the fact that God breathes into him the breath of life. Man is clay and breath, or, body and life. The principle of life which impregnates the body is called "soul." That which energizes the soul is the breath, or spirit, of God (see Isa. 42:5). Man is composed of body, soul, and spirit, not in the sense of three different parts, but all three united in one to make a living being, a person.

After God had created man he prepared for him in Eden a garden where all kinds of trees were planted. The term "Eden," which in Hebrew means "luxury, delight," may have suggested to the Israelite a place of beauty and fertility; it may also designate more specifically a geographical area in northwest Mesopotamia (see Ezek. 27:23). Among the trees in the garden are two of special importance (2:9). One is called "the tree of life . . . in the midst of the garden," whose fruit imparts immortality to those who eat it (3:22-24), and the other is "the tree of the knowledge of good and evil," whose fruit is forbidden to man (2:17; and 3:3, 5 where "the tree which is in the midst of the garden" is the tree of knowledge). The latter tree represents knowledge which God alone has and which he alone can give. That this special divine knowledge was believed to be concerned with moral judgments is shown by the phrase, "good and evil." Man is forbidden to eat of the fruit of this tree; that is, to acquire this knowledge which alone belongs to God and which he alone can give. Disobeying this command of God means death (2:17). The command to "till and keep" the garden (2:15) shows that work is not a curse, since sin had not yet come into the world. Work is part of the divine economy from the very beginning.

The description of the four rivers in verses 10-14 is a parenthetical section which breaks the sequence of thought in the narrative. The author is attempting to connect Eden with the world in which man lives. From Eden, we are told, there flows a mighty river to water the garden. It then divides into four branches which are called Pishon, Gihon, Hiddekel (Tigris), and Euphrates. The location of the first two rivers is uncertain; the last two are so familiar to the biblical writer that he has to say little or nothing to identify them. The source of these rivers lies to the north, in the mountains of Armenia, where we know the Tigris and Euphrates begin their long journey to the Persian Gulf. Eden, therefore, must be located to the north of Mesopotamia where the highest mountains in the world were thought to be (compare Gen. 8:4). This passage no doubt suggested the symbolic river of life with its healing and fructifying waters which is mentioned in Ezekiel 47 and Revelation 22:1.

Man is by nature a gregarious creature. He was created for fellowship, not for solitary loneliness. It became necessary, therefore, for God to provide a "helper fit for him" (2:18), to fill out his life in fellowship with one who corresponds to him in every way. This companionship was not found among the animals—the beasts of the field and the birds of the air—which God formed out of the ground (2:19-20). Even though the animals are formed out of the same ground as man, yet the writer emphasizes in several ways that man is superior to the animal kingdom. The fact that God himself did not breathe the breath of life into the animals, as he did when man was formed (2:7), is one indication that there is a closer relation between God and man than between God and the animals. Then, too, the fact that man gives names to the animals as they pass before him implies that he has authority over them, for he designates their character and determines their relation to himself (compare 1:28, where man's "dominion" over the animal kingdom is directly expressed).

When no suitable companion is found for man among the animals, God causes a deep sleep to fall upon Adam, takes a rib from his side, and "builds" (this is the literal meaning of the verb translated "made" in 2:22) it into a woman. The sheer joy of Adam when he sees woman for the first time is best expressed by the literal translation of the Hebrew text:

> "This is the moment! Bone of my bones,
> and flesh of my flesh" (2:23a).

"This moment," of course, contrasts with the earlier moment when the animals passed before Adam and no "helper fit for him" was found. Now there is one who answers to his needs, not only physically, but mentally and spiritually as well. Therefore "she shall be called Woman, because she was taken out of Man" (again there is a play on words in the Hebrew, in the words "woman" and "man"). The powerful sexual drive found in mankind is explained by the fact that God created man and woman so that, having come from one flesh, they are strongly moved to become one flesh again. Verse 24 answers the question of why a man will forsake his own parents and cling to his wife. Monogamy is rooted in the very order of the universe as created by God. Although Moses had to alter the divine plan and permit divorce because of sin (Deut. 24:1-4), Jesus argues against divorce in the New Age on the basis of this passage in Genesis (Matt. 19:3-9), and Paul sees in the union of man and wife the highest earthly expression of the ideal relationship between Christ and his Church (Eph. 5:31-32). Marriage belongs to God's pure creation from the beginning. There is nothing inherently wrong in the sexual attraction of man and woman. There is no cause for shame to exist between them in their nakedness, since sin and guilt are not yet present (2:25).

Sin and Its Results (3:1—5:32)

The Fall (3:1-7) [J]

"Now the serpent . . ." So begins the dramatic story of the battle for man's being. God had created man for fellowship with him. He had placed him in a beautiful garden and provided for all his needs. But into this idyllic scene comes a new actor, "the serpent," one of God's creatures, believed from ancient times to be endowed with special wisdom (Matt. 10:16; the Apocryphal book, Wisdom of Solomon 2:24, first identifies the serpent with the Devil; see also Rev. 12:9; 20:2). The serpent begins the attack with insidious sagacity and skill. He addresses his opening question to the woman, perhaps an indication that by nature and temperament she is regarded as more likely to fall prey to his wily ways. "Did God say, 'You shall not eat of any tree of the garden'?", he asks, knowing full well that he is distorting the divine prohibition (2:16-17), and sowing a seed of *doubt* in the woman's mind. Even though the woman is quick to point out the serpent's error as she notes how God had mercifully provided for all their needs, the words which she adds to the original prohibition—"neither shall you touch it"—seem to indicate a growing resentment at the restriction placed upon her and her husband. It is as though she were saying, "We can't even touch the tree which is in the midst of the garden!" The seed of doubt, sown by the serpent, is taking root in the heart of the woman. The first breach has been made in the rampart of man's being.

The frontal attack now begins. In his assertion, "You will not die" (3:4), the serpent *denies* the truth of God's warning in 2:17. Then he actually says that God had forbidden them to eat of the tree so that they would not share in his wisdom and become divine (3:5). After shattering the woman's faith in the authority and goodness of God, the serpent leaves the woman to ponder over his words. It does not take long for her to capitulate to the enemy. The tree with its hidden mysteries becomes suddenly attractive to the woman. She is strongly moved to eat of its forbidden fruit, because it "was good for food . . . a delight to the eyes, and . . . to be desired to make one wise" (3:6; see also I John 2:16, where the same three areas of temptation are mentioned). She must choose whether she wants to live in obedience to God's word and in dependence upon his goodness, or reach out and attempt to gain by her own ingenuity and strength the

things which God alone has the right to give. To become like
God, as the serpent insidiously puts it, is too much of a temptation for the woman to withstand and so she *disobeys* the word
of God. "She took of its fruit and ate; and she also gave some
to her husband, and he ate" (3:6; compare Phil. 2:6, where
Christ, the last Adam, in contrast to the first Adam, "did not
count equality with God a thing to be grasped"). The serpent
did his work well. Doubt and denial led to disobedience and
death. Man capitulated to the Evil One.

With the eating of the forbidden fruit, "the eyes of both were
opened" (3:7), as the serpent had said, but the knowledge they
receive is quite different from that which they had expected.
They know that they are naked; that is, they are no longer in a
state of innocence, but are conscious of their sinful state. The
shame which they experience as the result of their sin they try
to cover up by making girdles out of fig leaves (3:7).

The Curse (3:8-24) [J]

The perfect relationship between God and man is now broken.
Man must go his own way, forever hounded by his sense of guilt
and his inability to obey God. Servitude and anxiety take the
place of peace and happy freedom under God in the garden.

Because the man-made covering of fig leaves is inadequate to
conceal the shame and guilt of our first parents, they hide themselves from the presence of God as he walks in the garden in the
cool of the evening. In loving mercy God seeks them out and
asks them questions which give opportunity for self-examination
and acknowledgment of guilt. The first divine inquiry, "Where
are you?" (3:9), indicates that the perfect fellowship between
God and man has been broken. Man in his answer (3:10) fails
to give the reason for hiding from God in fear—his disobedience.
God presses the inquiry and the man finally acknowledges his
guilt, not, however, without attempting to incriminate the woman,
and even God himself. "The woman whom *thou* gavest to be with
me, *she* gave me fruit of the tree, and I ate" (3:12). The old game
of "passing the buck" goes back to Adam himself. The relation
between man and woman in their sinful state is quite different from
that which prevailed before the Fall. The man's exuberant joy at
seeing woman for the first time (2:23) now gives way to resentment and incrimination. He says, in effect, "That woman *there*, the
one you gave to me, *she* is the one who is the cause of all this trou-

ble!" Perfect communion with God and perfect community among men are impossible when sin enters the world.

The woman, questioned next, lays the blame upon the serpent who beguiled her (3:13). Since the serpent has no sense of guilt, God does not interrogate him, but proceeds immediately to pronounce a curse upon him. The order of events in this chapter is interesting. Sin had made its way into the world from the serpent, through the woman, to the man (3:1-7); God's inquiry started with the man, and proceeded to the woman, and then to the serpent (3:8-13); the divine judgment now falls in reverse order upon the serpent, the woman, and the man (3:14-19).

The serpent is the only one of the three to receive a direct curse from God (3:14). Its crawling movement on the ground and the fact that it seems to eat the dust (see Isa. 65:25) which man shakes from his feet are regarded by the writer of the story to be the result of the divine judgment. The natural enmity between man and the serpent (3:15) will not be removed until the Messianic Age (Isa. 11:8). This verse can be understood messianically only in the general sense that God overcomes sin in all its forms. The work of his divinely appointed Messiah becomes clear only in the New Testament.

The pains of childbirth and the subservient position of woman to man are the penalties she pays for her disobedience (3:16). The joyful promise of having children is overshadowed by the prospect of travail and sorrow. It is remarkable that in Genesis 1:28 the increase of the human race is the result of the divine blessing, whereas here it is connected with the curse of God upon mankind. Man himself escapes the direct word of judgment, which passes on to the ground, from which man came (2:7) and which produces the food which man eats. The close union between man and the ground is now broken by the curse, and the earth, of itself, produces "thorns and thistles" (3:18). Only by laborious toil can man make the ground yield the food he needs. Work is not a curse in itself (2:15), sin has made work a drudgery; and arduous toil and labor become a part of man's life because of the curse upon the ground. Even in the sentence of death, which is the result of sin (see Rom. 6:23), the mercy of God shines through, for he does not slay man at the moment of disobedience, but allows him to live until the breath of God leaves him and he returns to the dust from which he comes (3:19). The description of sin and its dire results is now finished, the sad story having been told in language which even a child can understand. The genius that clothes the most profound truths in picturesque symbols and images makes these stories particularly valuable for the teacher and for the student. To subject them to a rigid, literalistic method of interpretation not only defeats the purpose of the stories, but hopelessly obscures their true meaning.

Man now gives his wife a name (see 2:23, where she is designated merely as "Woman"). He calls her Eve, which is related to the verbal root meaning "to live." She is indeed the source of life, "the mother of all living" (3:20). This is truly an act of faith on the part of Adam. In the face of judgment and death, Adam expresses his belief that life will be triumphant in the end.

God's mercy toward sinful man is shown by the fact that he provides him with "garments of skins" (3:21). This provision for man implies the death of certain animals, which is sometimes regarded as the first allusion to sacrifice in Scripture.

The last three verses of this chapter (3:22-24) tell about the expulsion of man from the garden in Eden. According to God's original plan, man was to have been a gardener, taking care of the beautiful trees which God had planted, and living in complete dependence upon God's goodness (2:9, 15). Because of man's disobedience he is driven from the garden to become a different kind of worker. He now must till the soil himself and battle the weeds in order to eke out a precarious living for himself and his family. Anxiety and toil are man's lot for the rest of his days.

Combined with this rather melancholy description of man's condition on earth is the theological observation that man, because of his sin, is forever separated from the tree of life, and consequently from the possibility of obtaining immortality here on earth. The way to the tree of life is guarded by a revolving, flaming sword and the cherubim, or winged creatures with human heads, which represent the Deity on earth (see I Kings 6:23-28; Ezek. 1:5-14; 10:1-22). This way to the tree of life is not opened again until in the New Jerusalem God's saints eat "of the tree of life, which is in the paradise of God" (Rev. 2:7; 22:2).

The Story of Cain and Abel (4:1-16) [J]

The story of Cain and Abel shows how the sin of our first parents was passed on to their first-born, Cain, who murdered his brother Abel. A careful reading of this passage reveals an altogether different cultural setting from that which is found in the first three chapters of Genesis. For instance, the institution of sacrifice is taken for granted, since its origin and purpose are not explained, and the clan, with its laws of blood revenge, is already a well-established social unit. The building of a city (4:17) also presupposes a large sedentary population, which, by the way, helps to answer the perennial question, Where did Cain get his wife? The writer (J) does not intend to record all of the events of human history, nor is he giving a complete directory of all the people who ever lived. The main purpose of the story is to show the tragic consequences of man's first act of disobedience.

"Now Adam knew Eve his wife" (4:1). "To know" in Hebrew is not just an intellectual process. It means "to experience something or someone" in the fullest sense. "To know God," for instance, is not just to know about him intellectually; it is to know him in a saving way (Hosea 4:1; 4:6; Isa. 1:3). The highest and fullest expression of knowledge in the human realm is the love relation between husband and wife. It is in this sense that the word is used in Genesis 4:1. At the birth of Cain, Eve exclaims, "I have gotten [produced] a man with the help of the LORD." She is exuberant because she has given birth to a man-child, thus fulfilling her mission in the world as "the mother of all living" (3:20).

Abel's birth, on the other hand, is not heralded by a joyful oracle. Perhaps his very name, which means "breath, vapor," presages the tragic outcome of the story. The writer quickly gets to the point of the narrative by describing the offerings that the two brothers bring to the Lord. Cain, the farmer, brings "an offering of the fruit of the ground," whereas Abel, the shepherd, brings "of the firstlings of his flock and of their fat portions" (4:3b-4a). The reader is evidently supposed to know what a sacrifice is, and why and how it is offered.

For some reason, not told by the writer, "The LORD had regard for [literally, looked upon] Abel and his offering, but for Cain and his offering he had no regard" (4:4b-5a). Was Abel's sacrifice acceptable because it consisted of flesh? Yet the offering of the first fruits of the ground was acceptable to the Lord according to the Mosaic law (see Exod. 22:29). Perhaps there was something ritually improper in the way that Cain offered his sacrifice, but if that was so we are not told what the impropriety was. The reason probably lay in the spirit in which the sacrifices were offered (see Heb. 11:4). The very fact that the Hebrew text states that the Lord looked upon *Abel* first, and then upon his offering, and not upon *Cain* and his offering seems to indicate that the offerer, or at least the spirit of the offerer, is more important to the Lord than his offering. This, of course, is in line with the prophetic teaching on sacrifice (see Micah 6:6-8). When Cain becomes angry because God looked with favor upon Abel's sacrifice, and not upon his, he is warned to curb his anger. God tells him that sin, crouching like an animal at the door, is ever ready to spring upon a man and possess his soul entirely unless he is able to control it (4:7). Cain, however, rejects the divine counsel and lets jealousy and hatred so completely overpower him that he slays his brother.

In the questions which follow, God is giving Cain a chance to admit his guilt and receive divine forgiveness. But by the answers which Cain gives it appears that sin has gotten a firmer grip on him than it had on his father. Instead of evading the answer by making excuses, as Adam had done, Cain lies to God's face—"I do not know [where my brother is]"; and then he adds defiant words of insolence—"am I my brother's keeper?" (4:9). Again not only was true communion between God and man broken by sin (3:9), but also true community among men (4:9). The ideal order envisioned by God for man and this world was completely shattered. Over against this tragic picture we see what we might have been in Jesus Christ, the last Adam, who lived in perfect fellowship with God and loved his fellow men unto the end.

In consternation God says to Cain, "What have you done? The voice of your brother's blood is crying to me from the ground" (4:10). According to the law of blood revenge in ancient Israel a murdered victim was to be avenged by his next of kin, who was called "the avenger of blood" (Num. 35:19). Since, however, in this story Abel's brother is the murderer, the blood of Abel "screams" to the Lord for vengeance. The Lord, therefore, acts as the "kinsman-redeemer," and curses Cain, banning him from the ground which he, as a farmer, had cultivated for a living. The ground will no longer yield its fruit for Cain, and he is forever driven from before it to wander like a bedouin in the desert wastelands. As a wanderer he dwells in the land of Nod (the words for "wanderer" and "Nod" are similar in sound). Nod is vaguely described as being "east of Eden" (4:16).

Another conversation between Cain and God is recorded in verses 13-15, in which Cain, though not penitent, acknowledges that his punishment is too heavy for him to bear. In mercy God had spared his life, but now Cain is afraid that as a wandering nomad, unwanted and alone, he will lose his life at a stranger's hands. Away from home, and therefore presumably away from God (as, for example, II Kings 5:17), he feels unprotected in the unfriendly desert. Once again God shows his love for a man in sin by placing a sign on Cain which indicates that he belongs to God and that he is under his protection. "If any one slays Cain, vengeance shall be taken on him sevenfold" (4:15). Thus God becomes the "kinsman-redeemer" for the murderer as well as for the murdered (compare Paul's words in Romans 5:8, "But God shows his love for us in that while we were yet sinners Christ died for us"). Although Cain's fears for his life are thus allayed, he still wanders afar from home in the land of Nod with his uneasy conscience, a lesson for all who willfully rebel against God.

The Descendants of Cain (4:17-24) [J]

To the story of Cain, the wandering nomad, is joined the story of Cain, the city builder and progenitor of those who founded the various cultures and arts of ancient civilizations. The writer takes for granted that the earth is sufficiently populated to warrant the building of a city, and, incidentally, to provide a wife for Cain. A careful comparison of the genealogies in 4:17-18 (J) and chapter 5 (P) shows that they are apparently parallel forms of the same original listing of Adam's descendants. Cain and his line are described in 4:17-24 as the founders of primitive Eastern civilization. Cain and his son Enoch—not to be confused with the Enoch of chapter 5—are the originators of urban culture; Lamech is the first polygamist, whose boastful hymn of hate is the first poem in the Bible (4:23-24); Jabal is "the father of those who dwell in tents and have cattle" (4:20); Jubal is the originator of the musical arts; and Tubal-cain is the progenitor of those who work in metals. But man's moral condition does not improve with the great advance in culture. The brutal savagery of man is little affected by the thin veneer of civilization. According to Lamech's poem, in which he boasts of slaying a man for wounding him, the more humane *lex talionis*—the law of exact retribution for wrong—with its provision of taking *only* an eye for an eye, and *only* a tooth for a tooth, had not yet been thought of.

The Line of Seth (4:25-26) [J]

With Seth a new beginning is made. Cain and his descendants were thoroughly corrupted by sin. There was little hope for the

human race in that direction. God therefore established a new
line, beginning with Seth and leading directly to Noah (chapter
5). It was in the days of Enosh, the son of Seth, that "men began
to call upon the name of the LORD" (4:26), or, as we would say,
began to worship Yahweh. (The contrast between this passage
and Exodus 3:14 and 6:2-3, which seem to suggest that Yahweh
was first worshiped by the Israelites in the days of Moses, may be
more apparent than real. These passages may mean that the already
familiar name Yahweh was now invested with new meaning.)

The Line of Seth (5:1-32) [P]

Genealogies are the backbone of history. In biblical history
they are especially important, for they show that God reveals himself to people, particularly to his people, in the context of human
events. Thus the genealogies of Jesus, given in Matthew 1:1-17
and Luke 3:23-37, anchor in history the revelation of the Eternal
Word. The interest of this particular author in genealogies as the
framework of the history of salvation is shown by the fact that he
divides the history of the patriarchs into ten sections, each introduced by the word "generations" (5:1; see discussion of 2:4a).

The distinctive words of the story of man's creation found in
1:26-28 (P) meet us again in the opening verses of this chapter.
The words for "God," "created," "man," "likeness," and "blessed"
are the same in both passages. As a result of the divine blessing,
Adam, who had been created in the image of God (1:27), now
begets a son in *his own likeness*, according to *his own image*, and
he calls him Seth (5:3). The roll call of Seth's descendants includes Enosh, Kenan, Mahalalel, Jared, Enoch, who "walked with
God," Methuselah, who lived to be nine hundred and sixty-nine
years old and so is the oldest man in the Bible, Lamech, and Noah.

There seems to be some connection between the list of ten
antediluvian patriarchs found in this chapter and a list of ten
kings who ruled in Babylonia before the Flood, a list which appears in cuneiform sources. For instance, the seventh king of the
cuneiform list had special wisdom regarding the gods, which reminds us of Enoch, the seventh from Adam, who lived in close fellowship with God; and the tenth one in the cuneiform list is the
hero of the Babylonian Flood story, just as Noah, the tenth from
Adam, is the hero of the Hebrew Flood story. Such similarities can
hardly be accidental. But even more striking is the great age of the
antediluvian figures in both lists. According to the Babylonian list

the reigns of the kings extend anywhere from ten to sixty thousand years; in the Hebrew genealogy the life range of the patriarchs is a little short of a thousand years. The abnormal length of life ascribed to the Hebrew antediluvian heroes may, therefore, be due to Babylonian influence. Yet it is possible that this may be due to the tremendous vitality of man right after creation. It seems to be true that, as man moves away from this period, his life span gradually fades away to a mere threescore years and ten (see 6:3; Ps. 90:10).

In the biblical genealogy Enoch receives special attention because of his piety (5:21-24). It is twice said of him that he walked with God, that is, that he lived in close fellowship with God (see 6:9, where the same thing is said of Noah); he lived to be three hundred and sixty-five years old, the youngest in the line of Seth; and "God took him"—that is, God reached forth and drew him unto himself. In Jude 14 the writer specifically refers to Enoch "in the *seventh* generation from Adam," perhaps to emphasize by contrast the fact that in the line of Cain the seventh from Adam was Lamech (Gen. 4:18), a braggadocio, murderer, and bigamist. The Hebrew verb in the phrase "God took him," has in several places the special theological sense of being taken into the presence of God. It is used in the story of the translation of Elijah (II Kings 2:10), and twice in the Psalms in the general sense of being received by God after death (Pss. 49:15; 73:24). The greatest good for the Hebrew is to be with God. He alone is the giver of life—both in this world and the next. In the stories of Enoch and Elijah, God's greatest gift to man is fleetingly shown —life with him *which has no end*. In Christ the longing of man to be with God forever is assured for all who put their trust in him.

The notice of Noah's birth is accompanied by a word of hope. "Out of the ground which the LORD has cursed this one shall bring us relief from our work and from the toil of our hands" (5:29). Noah (whose name in Hebrew sounds like the verb meaning "to bring relief, to comfort, console") will in some way alleviate the heavy curse upon the ground (3:17) and bring about a new era when the Lord "will never again curse the ground because of man" (8:21). With the birth of Noah and his three sons, Shem, Ham, and Japheth, the stage is set for the Flood story.

The Flood Story (6:1—9:29)

Stories of a great flood or floods are found in many countries of the world. The Greeks, various ethnic groups in India, the island peoples of the Pacific, the Indian tribes of North and South America, and many others, have traditions of a devastating flood which covered the whole earth, or at least the land in which the story was current. Certainly the most ancient account of such a deluge is the one found among the peoples of the Mesopotamian Valley. This particular account, which has come down to us in several versions, is the one to which the Hebrew story is related.

According to the classical Babylonian narrative, which is preserved in a form known as the Gilgamesh Epic, Utnapishtim, a citizen of Shuruppak, which lies along the Euphrates, is advised by Ea, the lord of wisdom, to escape the flood that is to destroy his city. He is to build a ship in which he, his household, his belongings, and the cattle of the field will be saved. In accordance with Ea's word, Utnapishtim builds a ship and is saved from the ravaging waters. Like Noah, he sends out several birds to find out how far the waters have receded. When the ship finally rests on the summit of a mountain, Utnapishtim offers a sacrifice to the gods who gather around "like flies," and he and his wife are blessed with immortality. The resemblances between this story and the Genesis account of the Flood are too numerous to be accidental. The Hebrew writer must have been acquainted with the Flood story which was current in the Mesopotamian Valley as far back as 3000 B.C. Yet there are significant differences which reveal the unique way in which the biblical writers used this ancient material. The deep theological coloring of the Genesis story with its emphasis on divine judgment and grace, and its monotheistic conception of God, shows how the inspired Hebrews redeemed the material they received from other nations and made it a fit vehicle for the revelation of the true and living God.

In the biblical account itself there are differences in style and discrepancies in details which point to the composite nature of the narrative. For example, in 7:2, Noah is commanded to take "seven pairs of all clean animals . . . and a pair of the animals that are not clean" into the ark, whereas according to 6:19, "two of every sort" are to be taken into the ark. Then, too, in 7:12 and 8:2b the rains from heaven are the sole origin of the flood waters, whereas according to 7:11 and 8:2a, there is also a terrestrial disturbance which causes the fountains of the deep to burst forth. On the basis of these apparent discrepancies and certain characteristic phrases and points of view, it has become apparent that the Genesis account of the Flood is composed of two distinct literary traditions, designated by the letters J and P, which have been skillfully woven together to form the present biblical story. (See Introduction.)

The Semidivine Beings and the Daughters of Men (6:1-4) [J]

This difficult and fragmentary passage, the original purpose of which was to explain the existence of a gigantic race of semidivine beings, is used here by the writer to explain the increase of violence and corruption on the earth in the days before the Flood. Although it is not directly related to the Flood story, it serves as an excellent preface to verses 5-8, which tell of Yahweh's intention to destroy man from the face of the earth because of man's sinful nature. The basic narrative simply states that in the early days of the human race, the "sons of God," or semidivine creatures, married the daughters of men, and that from this illicit union there sprang a giant race called the Nephilim (see also Num. 13:33), who are identified with "the mighty men that were of old, the men of renown" (6:4). This story may lie behind the weird description of the "fallen mighty men of old" in Ezekiel 32:27, and it certainly is the source of the tradition of fallen angels who were punished by God when they "left their proper dwelling" (Jude 6; II Peter 2:4), although there is no reference to any punishment of the "sons of God" in the Genesis account. The writer (J) uses this ancient story not only to explain the increasing lawlessness and violence of mankind which lead to divine judgment upon the world by the Flood, but he is also probably indicating by the illicit marriage of supernatural creatures with human beings that evil is cosmic in nature, and therefore far more sinister than any mere defect in human nature. The difficult third verse of this passage has been translated in many ways, mainly because the meaning of the Hebrew verb, rendered "shall abide," is uncertain. The general meaning of the verse is clear, however. Divine judgment falls, yet God in his mercy did not destroy man at once, but allowed him a life span of one hundred and twenty years.

Corruption and Violence (6:5-8) [J], (6:9-12) [P]

The general account of the cosmic nature of sin found in 6:1-4 is followed by a more detailed description of the way sin has corrupted the nature of man and led to his alienation from God. "Every imagination of the thoughts of his heart was only evil continually" (6:5) is the gloomy verdict regarding man's spiritual condition. The eyes of God penetrate more deeply into the soul of man than any X ray. Man's heart, which in Hebrew psychology stands for the mind as well as the will, is completely corrupt in the sight of God. "And the LORD was sorry that he had made man on the earth, and it grieved him to his heart" (6:6). The ascription to the Deity of sorrow and remorse is in keeping with other passages of Scripture (for example, Hosea 11:8). God is so grieved at man's sinful condition that he resolves to wipe the human race from the face of the earth. As all forms of life were created for the benefit of man, according to the creation story, so in the Flood narrative all life, including "beast and creeping things and birds of the air" (6:7), must suffer in the divine judgment upon man.

"But Noah found favor in the eyes of the LORD" (6:8). Once again a ray of light penetrates the deep gloom of the preceding verses. In 3:20, immediately after the divine sentence of death upon man, Adam's faith in the ultimate victory of life is shown by his naming his wife Eve, "because she was the mother of all living." And then, immediately after Lamech's boastful hymn of murder and hate, the writer introduces Seth and Enosh as the ones who were the first to worship the true and living God under the name of Yahweh (4:26). Now again, after God decides to destroy the human race because it is so thoroughly wicked and corrupt, we read about one who is "a righteous man, blameless in his generation," who "walked with God" (6:9; see 5:22, 24). God's judgment is tempered by Noah's noble character. Again the mystery of divine grace! One belonging to the human order which is condemned to utter destruction is chosen by God to perpetuate that order. Judgment will come; punishment will be meted out; but the human race is not utterly destroyed (see also Hosea 11:9). "Violence" and "corruption," which are the marks of the days of Noah (6:11-12; see also Matt. 24:37), must be wiped out, yet in the midst of death the way to life is open.

The Flood (6:13—8:14) [J, P]

As has already been noted, the story of the Flood in Genesis stands in close literary relation to older flood stories from the Mesopotamian Valley. Although archaeology has brought to light accounts of a deluge in the Tigris-Euphrates Valley, no clear-cut evidence of Noah's flood has as yet been unearthed in Mesopotamia, in spite of fantastic claims to the contrary. It would seem then that the biblical account of the Flood, as well as the accounts of a flood found in Mesopotamia and other regions of the world, points to a catastrophe which took place as far back as the Stone Age. But whatever the historical antecedents of the biblical Flood story may have been, the abiding significance of the Genesis account lies in its deeply religious outlook and theological insights.

Even though the end of all flesh has come, God speaks with Noah, who is flesh (6:13). The purpose of God's conversation with Noah was to give him instructions concerning the building of the ark (6:14-16). It was to be constructed of gopher wood, evidently some kind of resinous material suitable for building ships, coated on the inside and outside with pitch, or more accurately bitumen, which was also used to calk the ship in the Babylonian story. Reckoning 18 inches to a cubit, the ark measured 450 feet long, 75 feet wide, and 45 feet high, about half as long and wide as the largest ocean liners today. According to the rather obscure terminology of verse 16, the ark was to be covered with a roof to protect it from the torrential rains, and have three decks with rooms or cabins for the occupants. After these instructions, there is the word of judgment upon all flesh (6:17), as well as the first mention of a covenant to be established between God and man (6:18; see 9:1-17 for a description of this covenant). All flesh is to be destroyed, according to God's word, yet "of every living thing of all flesh, you shall bring two of every sort into the ark, to keep them alive with you" (6:19). Again the mystery of grace!

The writer apparently knows of no distinction between clean and unclean animals before the Mosaic regulations were instituted, and so two of all flesh go into the ark with Noah. According to J's account, on the other hand, Noah takes with him seven pairs of clean and one pair of unclean animals (7:2). For J, the regulations concerning clean and unclean animals go back to the earliest times. Noah, who is wordless throughout the story, dutifully obeys God's command and enters the ark with his family—his wife, his three sons, and their wives, eight in all (see I Peter 3:20)—and the animals. "And the LORD shut him in" (7:16). The One who unleashes the raging waters gently closes the door of the ark to ensure the safety of those inside. By noting the exact dates of the Flood (7:11; 8:13-14), and other statistical data, the writer (P) is emphasizing the historical character of God's revelation.

"But God remembered Noah and all the beasts" (8:1). The sovereign Lord is mindful of his own. And he might well be in this instance, for the future of the human race and the divine plan of redemption ride with this frail bark. The waters subside and the ark rests on a mountaintop in Ararat (Urartu), known as Armenia today. The boisterous waves and wind had driven the ark to the mountainous region north of the Mesopotamian Valley. Noah sends forth the raven and the dove to determine how far the waters have receded. When the dove returns with an olive leaf, Noah knows that the waters of the Flood and the wrath of God have abated.

Noah's Sacrifice (8:15-19) [P], (8:20-22) [J]

God commands Noah to leave the ark and pronounces the creation blessing upon him (1:22, 28), since this marks a new beginning in the history of mankind. It is God who overarches the whole story of the Flood, giving the instruction to Noah, caring for him during the dangerous journey of the ark, and bringing him forth from the ark after his trying ordeal. In gratitude to the Lord for delivering him from the waters of death, Noah builds an altar as soon as he leaves the ark and offers burnt offerings unto the Lord (8:20). According to the Mosaic regulations these were sacrifices in which the whole of the victim was consumed upon the altar. That such offerings are thus represented as sacrificed long before they were instituted under Mosaic law is of no concern to J, who has little interest in the technicalities of religious observances.

The Lord, who is pleased with this spontaneous expression of Noah's gratitude, promises never to curse the ground again as he had done before (3:17; 4:12), or to destroy mankind in a worldwide catastrophe, even though man's innate depravity would continue to provoke and justify God's wrath (8:21). The sin of man, which no waters can wash away, is a challenge to God's mercy. God meets this challenge by assuring Noah that his daily needs will be met by the unbroken succession of "seedtime and harvest, cold and heat, summer and winter, day and night" (8:22).

God's Covenant with Noah (9:1-17) [P]

Before the detailed account of the covenant with Noah is given (9:8-17), the writer (P) reiterates the divine blessing upon Noah and his sons, reaffirms man's dominion over the animal kingdom, and introduces two new regulations which are to curb man's absolute authority (9:1-7). The creation blessing upon man (1:28) is now repeated as the human race enters a new chapter of history (9:1; see also 8:17). The single family of Noah is to replenish the whole earth, even as Adam and Eve were empowered to do in the creation story. "The fear of you and the dread of you shall be upon every beast of the earth . . . Every moving thing that lives shall be food for you; and as I gave you the green plants, I give you everything" (9:2-3). The animal kingdom was originally to be subject to man (1:26, 28); now it is in dread of him. Fear now rules the world. The peace and freedom which had existed between man and animal in the beginning is broken. The enmity between the serpent and man (3:15) now extends to the whole animal kingdom. This is a world of strife. Man kills animals for food, animals kill man, and man kills man! The peace of the garden, where man ate only "the green plants," is shattered forever. Only in the Golden Age will hostilities cease between man and animal, and man and man (Isa. 11:6-9; 2:4). God alone speaks the word of peace. Only in him can true peace be found (Jer. 6:14).

Even though this is a different world from the one God had originally intended, it is still God's world. He sets up certain regulations which govern and control man's relationships to man and to the animal kingdom. And man, though a sinner, still bears the mark of his divine Maker—"the image of God" (see 9:6)—as shown by his dominion over the animals (9:2) and by the sanctity of his life (9:6). Man has the right to kill any animal for food (9:3), but he must not eat the blood, "for the life of the flesh is in the blood" (Lev. 17:11), and all life is sacred in the eyes of God. The practice of eating flesh without the blood goes back to the times of Noah, according to P, and so is of universal significance. It is still observed by some Jews today (see also I Sam. 14:33-35). On the other hand, the animal which takes the life of a man shall be put to death (see Exod. 21:28), as well as the man who kills his fellow man. Man's life is inviolably sacred, since he was created in the image of God; it may not be taken without impunity either by animal or man. "Whoever sheds the blood of man, by man shall his blood be shed; for God made man in his own image" (9:6). The first part of this verse reads as poetry does in Hebrew. It is obviously very old and of great importance. It contains two regulations which are the basis of all social life. First, murder is to be punished with death. Blood for blood, life for life, is the penalty. The law of blood revenge, which is stated here in the simplest terms, was one of the stabilizing influences in ancient society. In spite of its severity—a life for a life—it was really a great blessing because it prevented society from degenerating into chaotic anarchy. The second stipulation is that *man* shall avenge the murder. By God's order man shares in the divine function of establishing and upholding justice on the earth. In early times the near kinsman was to put the murderer to death (see the discussion of 4:10); later, this became the duty of the state. It is significant that such a basic concept of the state does not emerge until after the Flood, when the world in its fallen state needs the restraining influence of law and order. Organized government, which acts as a dam against the flood of disorder, is a blessing from God, and should be respected by all men (see Rom. 13:1-7; I Tim. 2:1-3).

The Covenant which God makes with Noah (9:8-17) is a covenant of pure grace, universal and eternal. Like the divine promise of 8:22, it assures the stability of the natural order. "Never again shall all flesh be cut off by the waters of a flood, and never again shall there be a flood to destroy the earth" (9:11). God binds himself to the sinful world—not just to Israel—in a covenant relation. Although God's gracious promise is expressed in negative terms, it should be interpreted positively to mean that he will forever sustain and protect human life and the institutions he has ordained for the welfare and protection of human society. This Covenant should not be thought of as a provisional one, established on a temporary basis, to be superseded later by a different type of covenant. It is specifically called an "everlasting covenant" (9:16), and because it is based on God's word it can never be broken.

Even though God's word is all-sufficient assurance that he will keep his side of the Covenant agreement, he gives even further assurance of his faithfulness to weak and doubting man in the sign which he sets in the clouds. "I set my bow in the cloud, and it shall be a sign of the covenant between me and the earth" (9:13). The bow, a weapon of warfare, becomes a symbol of peace between God and man. When God's anger had passed with the Flood, he pointed to his bow in the clouds as the sign of his faithfulness.

The Curse Upon Canaan (9:18-27) [J], (9:28-29) [P]

The opening verses of this section conclude the Flood story of chapter 8 by stating that Noah and his three sons, Shem, Ham, and Japheth, went forth from the ark, and that from these three sons the whole earth was populated (9:18-19). Instead of going on to tell us who the descendants of these sons were, the writer inserts the rather indelicate account of Noah's drunkenness and his curse upon Canaan. Evidently there are two traditions represented here, one in which the three sons of Noah were Shem, Ham, and Japheth, and the other in which they were Shem, Japheth, and

Canaan. The writer tries to bring these two traditions together by inserting twice the statement that Ham was the father of Canaan (9:18, 22); but the tradition that Canaan was the youngest son (9:24) rather than Japheth, and that he received the curse rather than Ham, was the one which the writer chose for his purpose.

The main purpose of the story is not to pronounce a moral judgment on drunkenness, although the ill effects of excessive drinking are by no means absent in the story, but rather is to explain by the curse upon Canaan the immoral and degenerate character of the Canaanites as revealed particularly in their orgiastic religious rites. "Noah was the first tiller of the soil. He planted a vineyard" (9:20). Noah was not only an agriculturist; he also started a new venture in civilization—the cultivation of the vine, one of nature's noblest gifts to man. Although there are some warnings in the Old Testament against the excessive use of strong drink (for example, Isa. 5:11-12; Prov. 20:1; 23:29-35; 31:4-5), the Hebrews for the most part regarded the vine and its fruit as symbols of joy and blissful contentment (Pss. 104:15; 128:3; Micah 4:4; Zech. 8:12). Since Noah, the first viniculturist, was apparently unaware of the potency of his product, he is not blamed by the writer for his drunken condition. "Ham, the father of Canaan, saw the nakedness of his father, and told his two brothers outside" (9:22). The shameless look on his father's nakedness (see Lev. 18:6-20) is followed by shameless words, as Ham tells his brothers of his father's disgrace. In sharp contrast with the indelicate actions of Ham, Shem and Japheth respectfully cover the nakedness of their father with a robe. Now follow the words of an ancient poem in which Canaan, the youngest son—not Ham, the second oldest (6:10; 7:13)—is cursed by Noah, and Shem and Japheth are blessed (9:25-27). Canaan is degraded to the lowest position of servitude among his brethren; Shem, whose God is given the special name Yahweh ("LORD"), is to rule over Canaan; and Japheth, as a progenitor of the Gentiles, is to dwell in the bounds of Israel, evidently as an enemy alien. These ancient curses and blessings, which were thought to determine the future of a person or a people, quite accurately reflect the later history of Israel when she conquered the profligate Canaanites and made them subservient to her. The enemy alien within the borders of Israel may well refer to the Philistines who originally came from the islands of Greece, particularly Crete (or Caphtor; see Amos 9:7), and settled on the southern coastal plain of Canaan.

The Table of Nations (10:1-32) [P, J]

According to the Hebrews, all of the inhabitants of the world descended from the three sons of Noah. Shem was the father of the Semites (10:21-31), Ham was the father of the African peoples (10:6-14), and Japheth was the father of the Aryan or Indo-European peoples (10:2-5). Canaan, who is called the son of Ham, is the ancestor of the early inhabitants of Canaan, who were Semites (10:15-20). Although there are striking affinities between the Semitic and Hamitic language families, which reflect close racial ties in prehistoric times, the writer, in making Ham the father of Canaan, is probably referring more particularly to Egypt's long political and economic domination of Canaan. Even though certain sections of the world, like the Far East, are not included, since the Hebrews had no contact with them, the division of nations found here is quite convenient, and is still used to some extent by historians. The geographical area covered extends from Asia Minor (10:2-3) to Abyssinia (Cush, 10:6, or Ethiopia), and from Elam, east of Babylonia (10:22) to Greece (Javan, 10:2) and possibly even Spain (Tarshish, 10:4).

This chapter also has profound theological significance. It is the fulfillment of God's words of blessing to Noah and his sons in 9:1: "Be fruitful and multiply, and fill the earth." Although the writer (P) believes that all peoples come from one source, he also holds that the diversity of nations is the result of the divine blessing. The enriching, limitless power of God is shown in the vast number of nations on the earth, each with its own language and culture (10:5). Of even greater theological significance is the fact that God has called out of this multitude of nations a single people to be the recipients of his special revelation, that they may be the channel of his saving grace to the world. This is indicated by placing Shem, "the elder brother of Japheth" (10:21), and his descendants last in the chapter, after Japheth and Ham. Then, after the Tower of Babel story (11:1-9), which interrupts the sequence, the genealogy of Shem is resumed and carried through to Abraham. Thus the stream of "holy history"—that is, the revelation of God's redemptive purpose in history—is skillfully narrowed down to Abraham, the spiritual father of the Israelites.

This is indeed one of the most interesting chapters in Genesis. It is unparalleled among ancient documents for its accurate description and broad understanding of the geography, history, and culture of the world of that time. To discuss all the names recorded here is beyond the scope of this commentary. The figure of Nimrod, however, seems to warrant special attention, for he is presented as "the first on earth to be a mighty man" (10:8), "a mighty hunter before the LORD," whose prowess gave rise to a proverb: "Like Nimrod a mighty hunter before the LORD" (10:9). He is also regarded as one of the early founders of the great cities of Babylonia and Assyria (10:10-12). In spite of obscurities, it is clear that we are dealing here with a very ancient figure, who was the prototype of the mighty warrior kings of Babylonia and Assyria, often represented in art as enthusiastic hunters of wild game.

The Tower of Babel (11:1-9) [J]

This is not just an "explanation story" to tell us how the differences in human language arose. It also shows us how divine judgment is meted out to those who try to exalt themselves above God. "Now the whole earth had one language and few words" (11:1). In chapter 10 we have already learned that there were many nations in the world, each with its own language (10:5, 20, 31). According to the tradition found in chapter 11, however, mankind is still united and speaking one language. The people, who are represented as nomads, migrating from the desert to the fertile and cultivated areas, came into the valley of Shinar, or Babylonia, and settled there. When the writer notes that in this river valley bricks are used for stone, he may be deliberately pointing out the weakness of the structure which puny man is about to build. "Come, let us build ourselves a city, and a tower with its top in the heavens, and let us make a name for ourselves, lest we be scattered abroad upon the face of the whole earth" (11:4). Mankind intends to become famous by building a city and erecting a tower in it which will reach to heaven. The tower, because of its tremendous height, will attract people from everywhere, and thus it will become a symbol of the unity of all mankind.

There is little doubt that the building described here as "a tower with its top in the heavens" was one of the ziggurats, or terraced towers, found in Mesopotamia, which served as temples for the deities. Originally these pyramidal structures, built in successive stages, were thought to be a bond of union between earth and heaven, whereby the deity could come down to earth and the worshiper could ascend closer to his god—originally a noble thought expressed in architectural form. Therefore, condemnation of these cathedrals of the ancient world as merely symbols of man's pride and defiance of God is no more justified than would be the condemnation of Notre Dame Cathedral, or any church building with its spire reaching toward heaven. However, in later times, when the real significance of the ziggurat was forgotten, such massive towers, rising above the level plain of Shinar, became symbolic of the ruthless power and oppression of the great empires that existed in that region. In this way the Hebrew writer, vaguely familiar with the tradition of a lofty tower in Babylonia, came to interpret it as a symbol of man's pride and defiance of God.

So the Lord comes down to see the city and the tower! Mark the irony! Man's building, which he considers so big that it will touch the sky, is actually so small that the Lord must *come down* to see it. When the Lord sees that the tower is being successfully built because the people are united in their desire to become famous, he severely judges them by creating confusion in their language and scattering them "abroad from there over the face of all the earth" (11:8). The name Babylon, which means "gate of God," is here related to a Hebrew word of similar sound, carrying the idea of confusion (11:9). According to this tradition, therefore, diversity of languages came about as a divine judgment upon mankind because of man's pride and antagonism against God. In the Messianic Age the story of Babel is reversed, for, on the Day of Pentecost, with the outpouring of the Holy Spirit "men from every nation under heaven" hear of the mighty works of God in their own language (Acts 2:5-11).

Genealogy from Shem to Abram (11:10-32) [P, J]

Just as there were ten names in the genealogy from Adam to Noah, recorded in chapter 5 (P), so we find ten names in the genealogy from Shem to Abram. There is, however, an important difference between the two lists. In chapter 5 the span of life, except in the case of Enoch, was close to a thousand years, whereas in this section the duration of life diminishes gradually from 600 years for Shem to 148 years for Nahor, the father of Abram. It has already been noted that the farther man moves away from the time of creation the shorter his life span becomes.

Terah, like Noah (5:32), has three sons—Abram, Nahor, and Haran (11:26). Haran's son is Lot (11:27), the nephew of Abram. The name of Abram, which means "exalted father," is later changed to Abraham (17:5), which is said to mean "the father of a multitude of nations." Abram's wife is Sarai. Her name later is changed to Sarah (17:15), which means "princess." "Terah took Abram his son and Lot the son of Haran, his grandson, and Sarai his daughter-in-law, his son Abram's wife, and they went forth together from Ur of the Chaldeans to go into the land of Canaan; but when they came to Haran, they settled there" (11:31). According to this verse there are two stages in Abram's journey from Ur to Canaan. One is from Ur in the southern part of Babylonia to Haran in northwest Mesopotamia, a distance of about 550 miles. Here he sojourns until the death of his father Terah (11:32), after which he continues on to Canaan. It is strange that no reason is given for Abram's departure from Ur in Babylonia. It may be that he became dissatisfied with the religion of the Babylonians because of its many gods and low moral standards, and so he went forth in search for something that would satisfy the deep yearnings of his soul. The break he made with his pagan background must have been thorough and complete, for we do not hear a word about this early period of his life in the biblical story of his life. The tradition which connects Abram with Haran is much stronger than the one which derives him from southern Babylonia. In chapter 24, for instance, when Abram sends his servant to find a wife for his son Isaac, he directs him to go back to the old homestead in the city of Nahor (24:10), which is Haran, where the descendants of Nahor, the brother of Abram, are still living. Recent evidence from clay tablets unearthed at Mari, a city which flourished in northern Mesopotamia about 1750 B.C. and dominated the region around Haran, definitely links the patriarchs with this general area. It is quite certain that both of these traditions regarding the origins of the Hebrews are correct, since the Hebrew people are a combination of a number of racial elements.

PATRIARCHAL HISTORY
Genesis 12—50

The Abraham Story (12:1—25:18)

The Call of Abram (12:1-9) [J, P]

We are now moving out of the general, universal history of Genesis 1-11 into the particular history of God's Chosen People, which begins with the story of Abram. The last incident described in the pre-Abrahamic period was the building of the Tower of Babel, which ended on a sad and dismal note—". . . and from there the LORD scattered them abroad over the face of all the earth" (11:9b). What was to happen to these people who were dispersed throughout the world? Had the Lord given them up entirely? Was divine mercy finally exhausted? After Adam's sin God still allowed him to live, and even clothed him to cover his shame. After Cain's sin God mercifully put a sign upon him to protect him from wanton murder by those who did not know him. After the destruction of wicked men by the flood, God promised Noah that he would never destroy mankind again by such a great catastrophe, and he gave his bow in the clouds as a sign that he would be faithful to his Covenant promise. Up to this time God's mercy had always followed hard upon man's sin, to protect him from complete and utter annihilation. But now we hear no word of forgiveness, no word of mercy, no word of divine love. Yet all is not lost! Once again the words of God, as recorded in Hosea, come to mind: "I will not execute my fierce anger . . . for I am God and not man, the Holy One in your midst, and I will not come to destroy" (Hosea 11:9).

According to Genesis 12:1-3 God calls one man out from among the multitude of nations to be the channel of his saving grace to the world—Abram, who, like Noah, is a righteous man and upright in character. God calls him to be a blessing to "all the families of the earth." God has not forgotten mankind. The call of Abram is the logical, or should we say, the theological conclusion to Genesis 11:9. This is the saving link, as it were, between the wide-scale history of Genesis 1-11, and the "holy history" of Genesis 12 to the end of the Bible. God's redemptive purpose for the world now becomes focused on a specific person. God, who had dispersed mankind over the earth, now draws the nations unto himself through Abram and his seed. God will bless those who bless Abram—he will not forsake his own!

A new stage in the history of revelation has been reached in 12:1. God now speaks to one man, Abram, in the midst of the families of the earth. Why did he not choose to speak to Japheth, or Arpachsad, or Peleg, or someone else? The answer to this question is not given in the biblical account. Divine election is entirely a matter of God's grace and wisdom. It is not our function to question God in these matters (Job 9:12). God's word

not only creates the world, it also directs the saving acts and ac-
tors of history through which the world is to be saved. He calls
Abram, and Israel (Exod. 19:5-6), and his Servant (Isa. 42:6)
to bring salvation to all mankind.

But the call of God demands a response on the part of man. It
is not easy to follow God. Often the real reason people do not
believe in God is that they do not want to obey him. Abram is
asked to leave country, relatives, and family and go "to the land
that I will show you" (12:1). He is to rely entirely upon God
(Heb. 11:8). If Abram obeys, God will *bless* him. This is the key
word in God's promise. It occurs five times in two verses (12:
2-3). The promise, "I will make of you a great nation, and I will
bless you" (12:2), springs from the creation blessing (1:28).
God himself will now give Abram the great name (12:2) which
man had previously tried to gain for himself without success
(11:4). God's blessing (12:3; note the plural, "those who bless
you") outstrips the divine curse (singular, "him who curses you";
see also Exod. 20:5), showing the limitless extent of divine mercy.

"So Abram went" (12:4). In a simple word, "and he went"
(one word in Hebrew), the writer describes the act of silent
obedience that changed the course of world history. The long
hours of pondering and meditation, the fateful moment of decision, the days of preparation before the final departure, and
then the final farewell to home and friends and all that had been
his life—all of this is summed up in one word, "and he went."
If Terah died before Abram left Haran, as one would naturally
assume from the text, there is some discrepancy between the
figures found in 11:26, 32 and in 12:4. This may result from the
inclusion of several divergent strata of tradition in the narrative.

Lot, who goes along with Abram, figures prominently in the
events recorded in chapters 13 and 19. "When they had come to
the land of Canaan, Abram passed through the land to the place
at Shechem, to the oak of Moreh" (12:5-6). Shechem is situated
on the eastern side of the pass between Mount Ebal and Mount
Gerizim in central Palestine. It was already an ancient center of
religious activity when Abram came upon it, for it is referred to
as the site of "the oak of Moreh," or "the oak of teaching, or
teacher," which must have been an ancient sacred tree from
which oracles were obtained (see Gen. 35:4; Deut. 11:30;
Joshua 24:26; Judges 9:37). Here God appears to Abram and
says, "To your descendants I will give this land" (12:7). Abram

is now assured by God that he has reached the goal of his pilgrimage, and so he builds an altar to the Lord, in whose name he proceeds to take possession of the land.

From Shechem, Abram moves southward along the ancient highway on the central mountain ridge of Palestine to the Bethel-Ai region. Bethel, mentioned more times in the Bible than any other city except Jerusalem, was originally called Luz (28:19). It is situated about ten miles north of Jerusalem. Ai was the site of an ancient ruin about two miles southeast of Bethel (see Joshua 7:2-5). It was in this area that Abram spread his tent, built an altar, "and called on the name of the LORD" (12:8). From here "Abram journeyed on [literally, "pulled up stakes"], still going toward the Negeb," that is, the south (12:9).

So far, the wanderings of Abram in Canaan can be traced by the altars he builds. The altar and the tent, in fact, may be thought of as symbols of Abram's life, the altar representing his fellowship with God, the tent representing his earthly pilgrimage from place to place, in utter reliance upon God. As the writer of Hebrews says, Abraham was "living in tents . . . For he looked forward to the city which has foundations, whose builder and maker is God" (Heb. 11:9-10). It is significant that there is no reference to Abram's building an altar while he is sojourning in the Negeb or when he goes down into Egypt (12:10-20). Perhaps this may have something to do with Abram's moral lapse in Egypt described in the following verses.

Abram in Egypt (12:10-20) [J]

Because of a severe famine, which is a common occurrence in Canaan (see Ruth 1:1; Amos 4:6-9), Abram and Sarai go down to Egypt, the granary of the ancient world (see 42:1), "to sojourn there" (12:10; similar incidents are also described in chapters 20 and 26). The infiltration of Egypt by groups of nomadic Semitic people from the north was also a common occurrence in early times. In fact, a tomb painting from Beni-hasan in Egypt, dating from about 1900 B.C., the time of Abram, shows a family of Semites with their possessions being introduced by two Egyptian scribes to some high official of the Egyptian government. Because of Sarai's great beauty, Abram suggests to her that she pose as his sister when they get to Egypt, for he knows that "when the Egyptians see you, they will say, 'This is his wife'; then they will kill me, but they will let you live. Say you are my sister, that it may go well with me because of you, and that my life may be spared on your account" (12:12-13). In other words, Abram is evidently willing to endanger his wife's honor in order to save his own life. By this subterfuge, to which Sarai apparently agrees, Abram's life is spared, and he is handsomely rewarded by the Pharaoh for Sarai's sake (12:16). A highly imaginative description of the beauty of Sarai may now be read in the newly discovered "Genesis Apocryphon" (Col. XX), which was found among the manuscripts at Qumran, and which is dated anywhere from the fourth to the second century B.C.

But why should Abram act in this despicable way? One thing is certain: the Old Testament writers do not whitewash their heroes. The main purpose of the history of Abram is to portray him as the ideal righteous man, the hero of faith who obeys God and trusts him implicitly. Yet in this story he lacks the very qualities which he is supposed to exemplify. Even though Sarai was his half-sister, according to 20:12, he was untruthful in denying that she was his wife. But even more shameful was the fact that he lied to save his own life, and then accepted a bounteous reward in exchange for his wife's honor.

It is at this point, when the divine promise is imperiled because of Abram's dismal failure, that God steps in to rescue him and his wife. "But the LORD afflicted Pharaoh and his house with great plagues because of Sarai, Abram's wife" (12:17). God's power is described here as extending beyond the borders of Canaan into Egypt itself. Pharaoh and his family are stricken with a great misfortune from the Lord. The Egyptian ruler immediately knows—we are not told how or why—that this has come upon him because of Sarai. Pharaoh thereupon commands Abram to take his wife and possessions and leave the country, which Abram promptly does, under military escort.

Abram and Lot Separate (13:1-18) [J, P]

After Abram's lamentable experience in Egypt, he returns to Canaan with his family and possessions. Disgraceful as his conduct had been in Egypt, he now seems determined to make a new start by going back again to Bethel, "to the place where his tent had been at the beginning, between Bethel and Ai, to the place where he had made an altar [the Hebrew here also has the phrase, "at the beginning"]; and there Abram called on the name of the LORD" (13:3-4). Nowhere in Egypt did we hear of

Abram's building an altar or calling on the name of the Lord. There he had been entirely on his own, living by his own ingenuity, not by faith in God. But now he gets back on the track. Again he takes up the life of fellowship and faith, symbolized by the altar and tent which had been at Bethel at the beginning.

The main subject of this chapter is the separation of Lot and his herdsmen from Abram and his herdsmen (13:5-13). The flocks of these two families had become so numerous that "the land could not support both of them dwelling together" (13:6). When strife actually breaks out between the herdsmen of Abram and Lot, Abram, the older, gives Lot, the younger, the opportunity of choosing any portion of the land for himself and his flocks. Lot, whose eyes were focused on this world and the things around him, looks down from the mountain height on which Bethel is situated and beholds the well-watered plain of the Jordan before him. So green and fertile was this region extending southward to the Dead Sea that the writer compares it to "the garden of the LORD" (the Garden of Eden) and "the land of Egypt," which was irrigated by a river and was noted for its fertility. Unable to resist the lure of this fertile region, in spite of his uncle's prior claim and the evil character of the people who lived there (13:13), Lot selfishly chooses the plain of the Jordan for his family and flocks. The reference to the wickedness of the people of Sodom prepares the way for the account of the overthrow of the Cities of the Plain in chapter 19. Lot, who "moved his tent as far as Sodom" (13:12), is next found living in Sodom (14:12; 19:1). He had succumbed completely to the temptations so often associated with material prosperity.

In sharp contrast with Lot, the man of this world with its fleeting rewards, is Abram, the man of faith, who is blessed by God with an eternal reward. The Lord says to Abram, after he had so generously given the best of the land to Lot, "Lift up your eyes, and look from the place where you are, northward and southward and eastward and westward; for *all the land* which you see I will give to you and to your descendants for ever" (13:14-15). God's reward to the man of faith and his seed is the whole Promised Land. Abram is to walk up and down throughout this land and claim it in faith for his descendants. Abram now settles down "by the oaks of Mamre, which are at Hebron" (13:18), where he builds an altar to the Lord, and where the events of the following chapters are assumed to have

taken place (14:13; 18:1). Hebron, which lies some twenty miles
south of Jerusalem, was established about 1700 B.C. according
to the information recorded in Numbers 13:22, which would
have been sometime after the days of Abram. It is for this
reason, therefore, that in the story Abram is associated more particularly with the oaks of Mamre, and "Hebron" is added to explain where Mamre was (13:18; 23:19).

Abram Wars with Four Eastern Kings and Meets Melchizedek (14:1-24) [?]

This is the most enigmatic chapter in the saga of Abraham. In
the other chapters of the story, Abram usually appears in the
opening verses as the main character of the episode, but here he
is not introduced until the thirteenth verse, when he is described
as "Abram the Hebrew," as though he had never been mentioned
before. Nowhere else is Abram pictured as a hard-riding, hard-
hitting warrior, capable of overcoming, with 318 men, the combined armies of four kings (probably tribal chiefs). The identification of the four kings of 14:1 is still uncertain.

The latest word on this most difficult problem is as follows.
The old theory that Amraphel of Shinar (Babylon) was Ham-
murabi, the famous king of Babylon (about 1728-1686 B.C.), is
no longer tenable. The name Arioch has been equated with that
of Arriwuk, the son of Zimri-lim of Mari (about 17th century
B.C.). Chedorlaomer, the king of Elam, and leader of the coalition, has been identified as Kuter-Naḫḫunte, a king of Elam
who ruled toward the end of the 17th century B.C. And it has
been suggested that Tidal, king of Goiim, is the same as Tudḫalia
I, king of the Hittites, also in the 17th century B.C. Even if these
identifications were conclusive, they would still pose a problem,
for they would indicate that Abram lived sometime in the 17th
century B.C., whereas most scholars today are of the opinion that
he lived about 1900 B.C. The problem therefore remains unsolved.
Finally, the section about Melchizedek (vss. 18-20) obviously interrupts the account of Abram's meeting with the king of Sodom
(vss. 17, 21-24). According to this ancient literary fragment, the
high regard for Jerusalem as the political and religious center of
Israel extends back to patriarchal times.

In spite of these problems and uncertainties, the general
validity of the background of Genesis 14 has been amazingly

corroborated by archaeological explorations in Transjordan and the Negeb of Palestine. The road which the four kings presumably used in their invasion of Transjordan, the ruins of cities they destroyed (14:5-6), and the trail of destruction they left across the Negeb have all come to light in recent years through the untiring efforts of Professor Nelson Glueck. In a word, archaeological evidence agrees with the literary tradition of Genesis 14.

According to the story of this chapter, four kings of the East march westward to quell the riot of five petty kings whose cities are located at the extreme southern end of the Dead Sea. After a circuitous route, which takes the invaders as far south as the Gulf of Aqaba and then northwest to Kadesh-Barnea, they meet the rebellious coalition of five kings in the Valley of Siddim— mentioned only in this chapter—and defeat them utterly, taking "all the goods of Sodom and Gomorrah, and all their provisions," and going their way (14:11). It is at this point that the Abram-Lot tradition is rather clumsily attached to the account of the invading kings: "they also took Lot, the son of Abram's brother, who dwelt in Sodom, and his goods, and departed" (14:12). When Abram is told about Lot's capture, he pursues the armies of the four kings, defeats them in the vicinity of Damascus with a handful of men, 318 in number, and rescues Lot and his family and their possessions. On the way back from his victory over Chedorlaomer, Abram is met by the king of Sodom at the Valley of Shaveh or King's Valley (14:17), which by tradition is located in the vicinity of Jerusalem (see II Sam. 18:18). At this point the Melchizedek episode interrupts the narrative, which resumes again at verse 21.

Melchizedek is the priest-king of Salem, which probably stands for Jerusalem (see Ps. 76:2). Melchizedek, an old Canaanite name meaning "my king is Zedek" (the name of a deity), probably suggested to the Hebrews something like "my king is righteousness," or "king of righteousness." As priest of the God Most High he blesses Abram for his chivalrous action in saving Lot and his family from the invading forces, and in turn receives tithes of the spoils from Abram. By receiving this blessing and giving tithes, Abram, the servant of Yahweh, the God of Israel, recognizes Melchizedek's faith in the one true God Most High. In verse 22 Abram actually swears by the name of Melchizedek's God, who is identified with Yahweh—"The LORD God Most High." The solemnity of the Melchizedek story is in sharp contrast with the purely mundane level of the transaction between the king of Sodom and Abram.

Melchizedek is mentioned in only two other places in Scripture—Psalm 110:4 and Hebrews 5-7. In Psalm 110 the ideal King of Israel, God's Anointed One, or Messiah, is being described. As in Psalm 2, God will give him victory over all of his enemies. But in Psalm 110 we learn something new about God's king. He will also be a priest, discharging priestly functions as a king. "The LORD has sworn and will not change his mind, 'You are a priest for ever after the order of Melchizedek' " (Ps. 110:4). The ancient priest-king of Jerusalem is, therefore, the ideal example of God's Anointed One whom he will set over Israel.

The writer of the Letter to the Hebrews, following in the same line of thought, makes Melchizedek, the ideal priest-king, the type of Christ. His argument, extending over three chapters (5-7), is rather long and complicated, but his main point is clear. Christ's priesthood is better than that of Levi, since Christ is the Son of God, eternal, "holy, blameless, unstained, separated from sinners, exalted above the heavens" (Heb. 7:26). In the Old Testament, Abram paid tithes to Melchizedek and was blessed by him. Since Levi was in the loins of Abram "one might say that Levi himself . . . paid tithes through Abraham" (Heb. 7:9). Therefore Melchizedek's priesthood must have been better than Levi's, if Levi, through Abraham, paid tithes to Melchizedek. Hence, Melchizedek, who is of a higher order than Levi, is a type of Christ, the perfect High Priest of the one true and living God.

The last four verses of the chapter conclude the conversation between the king of Sodom and Abram. "Give me the persons, but take the goods for yourself," is the offer of the king of Sodom to Abram for his daring feat (14:21). Abram, however, in a noble spirit refuses the offer, since he had not made war to gain riches, and he did not want to be under obligation to the king of Sodom and the people of the Plain. All he asks is that his followers be given their rations which they had consumed on the campaign and that his three allies, "Aner, Eshcol, and Mamre," be given their share of the booty (14:24).

God's Covenant with Abram (15:1-21) [J, E]

The divine promises and blessings of 12:1-3 and 13:14-17 are now reiterated for Abram as he fearfully faces the future alone and childless. Couched in terms that are reminiscent of the prophetic literature (see 20:7, where Abraham is called a prophet), the "word of the LORD" comes to Abram "in a vision," assuring him of divine protection ("I am your shield"), and promising him that his reward—that is, his posterity and the possession of the land—will be very great (15:1). This promise seems to stir up even greater anxiety in the heart of Abram, for he cries out, "O Lord GOD, what wilt thou give me, for I continue childless, and the heir of my house is Eliezer of Damascus?" (15:2). The difficult Hebrew phrase, translated "and the heir of my house," should probably be rendered, with slight change in the Hebrew text, "and the son of Meseq (that is, Damascus) is the son of my house," with the added phrase for explanation, "that is Eliezer of Damascus." "Behold, thou hast given me no offspring; and a slave born in my house will be my heir" (15:3). Abram's main worry is that he is without an heir from whom the Covenant people will spring. In such a situation, a slave of the household could be adopted and become the heir of the adopter. This was in accordance with the law of the land, as we know now from ancient texts discovered recently in Nuzu, a city in northern Mesopotamia, which throw a flood of light upon the social customs of this area in the second millennium B.C., and actually explain a number of patriarchal laws and practices described in Genesis. These Nuzu texts also declare that if a son is born to the adopter after he has adopted a slave to be his heir, the adopted son must yield his place as heir to the adopter's own son. This is implied in verse 4 of the passage. "And behold, the word of the LORD came to him, 'This man shall not be your heir; your own son shall be your heir.' "

To give Abram further assurance, God directs him to try to count the stars in the sky. "So shall your descendants be" (15:5). Abram believes God, even though from the human point of view the fulfillment of such a promise seems impossible. It was this trust in God when the future seemed hopeless that made Abram the hero of faith for all time to come. "And he believed the LORD; and he reckoned it to him as righteousness" (15:6). Because of Abram's act of faith by which he gave himself completely into God's hands, God declared him to be righteous— that is, to be in right relation with him. This righteousness which God reckoned to Abram was entirely dependent on *faith* in God and not on the works of the Law, for the Law was not in existence in Abram's day. Thus Paul could use Abram's personal faith in a personal God as the supreme illustration of the faith needed by a Christian in order to be saved (Rom. 4; Gal. 3). God declares us righteous, that is, in saving relation with him, when we trust implicitly in Christ for our salvation.

The second assurance, namely, the possession of the land, is sealed by a Covenant (15:7-21). This seems to be a different occasion from the one described in verses 1-6. According to verse 5 it was night when Abram went forth to see the stars; here it is evening, "as the sun was going down" (15:12). In spite of Abram's profound faith described in verse 6, he nevertheless questions the divine promise regarding the land: "O Lord GOD, how am I to know that I shall possess it?" (15:8). God does not give a direct answer to this query, but commands Abram to prepare certain animals for a covenant-making ceremony. God in his mercy enters into a *Covenant* relation with Abram to assure him of his faithfulness to his word.

This is a most significant passage, for it is the only place in Scripture where this particular ceremony is described in detail. This Covenant sacrifice is alluded to, however, in Jeremiah 34:18: "And the men who transgressed my covenant and did not keep the terms of the covenant which they made before me, I will make like the calf which they cut in two and passed between its parts." The animals were to be killed and divided "and laid each half over against the other; but he did not cut the birds in two" (15:10; see Lev. 1:17). In the ceremony the two contracting parties then passed between the rows, symbolizing their unity, as well as the fact that if one violated the agreement, he would be slain like the animal victims (so Jer. 34:18).

The screeching birds of prey, attracted by the carcasses, are driven off by Abram. The extraordinary elements, so vividly described—the screeching birds, the horror of great darkness, the deep sleep, and the lurid appearance of smoke and fire, representing the presence of the Deity passing between the divided portions of the carcasses—all emphasize the mysterious solemnity of the act. The promise of the land, described and ratified in verses 18-21, is preceded in verses 13-16 by a prediction of the bondage in Egypt and the Exodus. Even though Abram himself will not fully possess the land, his descendants will return with great possessions and claim it for themselves.

Hagar and Ishmael (16:1-16) [J, P]

The curse of Sarai's barrenness has hung heavily over Abram's life ever since their marriage (11:30). In spite of the divine assurances that he would have descendants as numerous as the dust of the earth (13:16) and the stars of the sky (15:5), Abram again shows a lack of faith in God by taking Sarai's Egyptian handmaid to wife in order to have a child. The evidence for the legality of this practice again comes from the Nuzu texts, where it is specified in marriage contracts that if a wife is childless she must provide her husband with a slave wife. "And he went in to Hagar, and she conceived; and when she saw that she had conceived, she looked with contempt on her mistress" (16:4). Sarai naturally becomes jealous at this turn of affairs and drives Hagar from the house.

Even though Abram is within his legal rights in taking Hagar to wife, the practice of bigamy under any circumstances does not create a happy situation in a home (see I Sam. 1:6). Our sympathies are with Hagar as she flees from the jealous wrath of Sarai and wanders, lonely and helpless, in the desert. She was evidently making her way toward Egypt, her homeland, for "the angel of the LORD found her by a spring of water in the wilderness, the spring on the way to Shur" (16:7; see 20:1; 25:18). The way of Shur, which Hagar had taken, has now been identified; it extended from Beer-sheba to Sinai, and thence to Egypt, and served as an important caravan route in biblical times through the Negeb to the border of Egypt. The Angel of the Lord tells Hagar that she is to have a son and that his name is to be Ishmael (meaning, in Hebrew, "God hears"), "because the LORD has given heed to your affliction" (16:11). The Angel of the Lord, mentioned here, is a manifestation of Yahweh. Several times the Angel is identified with the Deity, speaking and acting as God himself (see 16:10; 21:18; 22:15-18). This manifestation of God, apparently in human form, though limited in the Old Testament to few occasions of short duration, is of deep theological significance. It anticipates the full revelation of God in Jesus Christ who became flesh and dwelt among us.

The site of the well, where Hagar rested, receives its name from this theophany. The Hebrew name, Beer-lahai-roi (16:14), which is impossible to translate with absolute certainty, probably denoted originally the place where the living, seeing God dwelt.

According to the popular tradition, however, reflected in Hagar's explanation of the name (16:13), it means the place where she saw God and lived, thus indicating that she was especially favored, for no man ever saw God and lived (see Exod. 33:20; Judges 13:22). The fact that God should look upon Hagar, a despised and rejected foreign slave, is indeed a wonderful thought. Even though Hagar can never become the mother of the son of promise, God mercifully watches over her as she leaves Abram's house and wanders out into the desert. So God's eyes follow all mankind, protecting and providing for all of his children. Truly he is the God of seeing!

Although the writer does not mention it specifically, Hagar must have returned to face the insults and jealous glances of Sarai, for we are told that "Hagar bore Abram a son; and Abram called ... his son, whom Hagar bore, Ishmael" (16:15).

The Covenant with Abraham and the Institution of Circumcision (17:1-14, 23-27) [P]

The priestly account of the establishment of the Covenant between God and Abraham is told in a fashion different from J's account, recorded in chapter 15. The name by which God reveals himself to the patriarch in chapter 17 is El Shaddai (see Revised Standard Version footnote), translated "God Almighty" (17:1; see also 28:3; 35:11; 43:14; 48:3). According to Exodus 6:3, God says to Moses, "I appeared to Abraham, to Isaac, and to Jacob, as God Almighty, but by my name the LORD I did not make myself known to them." "Shaddai" was the "God of the Fathers," whom the patriarchs deliberately chose as their Deity. The name means "the Mountain One," which implies that originally Shaddai was a mountain deity, whose home probably was thought to be in Northern Mesopotamia. The English rendering, "Almighty," is based on the translations of the term in the older versions of the Old Testament. In this chapter the duties involved in the Covenant relationship are emphasized. God says to Abram, "Walk before me, and be blameless" (17:1), which means that Abram is to live a life completely dedicated to God, thus meriting his favor and blessing. God then makes a covenant with Abram (the Hebrew of 17:2 reads, literally, "I will give my covenant"), promising to multiply his seed. It should be noted that, according to this chapter, God executes his Covenant with Abram only through his word, whereas in chapter 15, an elaborate ceremony accompanies the ratification of the Covenant. Abram's acceptance of the Covenant agreement is indicated by the fact that Abram bows in humility and reverence before God (17:3a). In verses 3b-8 the Covenant agreement is repeated with two major additions. Abram's name is changed to Abraham, which is a sign of the patriarch's new Covenant relation with God, and to the new name is added the promise that he will be "the father of a multitude of nations," which phrase, according to the writer, is to be regarded as the etymological explanation of the word Abraham (17:5). Actually, however, the two forms, Abram and Abraham, are variant spellings of the same name.

The other new element introduced in this section is found in verse 7: "And I will establish my covenant between me and you and your descendants after you throughout their generations for an everlasting covenant, to be God to you and to your descendants after you." According to this statement, the Covenant relationship is not only between God and Abraham, but also between God and Abraham's descendants, which means that it is to be an everlasting Covenant (see 17:13,19). God, of course, was always faithful to the Covenant agreement, but Israel—that is, the descendants of Abraham—broke their Covenant vows again and again throughout their history. The Mosaic Covenant (Exod. 19-24), the renewal of the Covenant under Joshua (Joshua 24:25), and the New Covenant (Jer. 31: 31-34) all testify to God's persistent love for Israel even though she was rebellious and unfaithful. The "better covenant," mediated by Christ, is also an eternal Covenant (see Heb. 8:6; 13:20).

The external sign of the Abrahamic Covenant is circumcision (17:9-14). It is to be performed on the eighth day after birth upon all male members of the household, including slaves born in the house and those bought with money. Thus the blessings of the Covenant relation are not limited to Abraham and his descendants alone. The rite of circumcision, which was a widespread custom long before the days of Abraham, was stamped in Israel with special religious significance. It was the outward sign of membership in a community of faith, with all of the privileges pertaining thereto. The rite of circumcision has been faithfully observed in the Jewish community down through the centuries. The prophets later spiritualized the practice, teaching that the outward sign of circumcision should represent the true dedication of the heart to God (see Jer. 4:4). In compliance with God's command, Abraham circumcises all the male members of his household, including Ishmael, who, we are told, was thirteen years of age at the time (17:23-27).

The Promise of a Son (17:15-22) [P]

This account of the promise of a son, which is paralleled in 18:1-5, begins with God's statement to Abraham that his wife's name shall be changed from Sarai to Sarah (17:15). No etymological explanation of the new name is given. Sarah is simply a variant spelling of Sarai. As in the case of Abraham (17:5), the new name accompanies the divine blessing: "I will bless her, and moreover I will give you a son by her; I will bless her, and she shall be a mother of nations; kings of peoples shall come from her" (17:16). The divine blessing which was pronounced upon Adam and Eve to make them fruitful (1:28), now brings fruitfulness to Sarah's barren womb. The incredulous laughter of Abraham on hearing the news that he was to have a son should be compared with the laughter of Sarah in 18:12. "Shall a child be born to a man who is a hundred years old? Shall Sarah, who is ninety years old, bear a child?" (17:17).

Abraham cannot believe that Sarah will bear a child, and so he pleads with God that Ishmael may live in his sight and enjoy divine protection, so that he may be the one through whom the promises made to Abraham will be fulfilled. But God is adamant. His way, which is many times inscrutable to human eyes, must prevail. Sarah will bear a son whose name shall be Isaac (the name means in Hebrew "he laughs"), reminiscent of Abraham's laughter when he first heard the incredible news (17:17). In response, however, to Abraham's prayer, God promises that Ishmael will become the father of a great nation (17:20). Even though Ishmael is rejected as the son of promise, God does not forsake him. God never cuts off his children entirely. "But I will establish my covenant with Isaac, whom Sarah shall bear to you at this season next year" (17:21). God's purpose will be realized. Neither man nor nature can thwart it.

The Promise of a Son (18:1-15) [J]

"And the LORD appeared to him by the oaks of Mamre, as he sat at the door of his tent in the heat of the day" (18:1). The careful attention to details is characteristic of J. In a few words he paints the background of the story—the oaks of Mamre near Hebron, the tent by the side of the road, Abraham sitting by the door, the hot noonday sun, and then the sudden appearance of the Lord! After this introductory statement, Abraham greets three men who appear before him by bowing himself to the ground in true oriental fashion and offering to them his generous hospitality. Throughout this episode and the events which follow in this and the following chapter, the relationship of Yahweh to the three men who visit Abraham is difficult to determine. According to the Hebrew text Abraham addresses his three visitors, "Oh Lord," as though he already recognized Yahweh. With slight change in the Hebrew text, the term can also mean "My lords," referring to the three men as human beings, or "My lord" (as in the Revised Standard Version, 18:3), perhaps addressing the most distinguished of the three visitors, but not recognizing him as Yahweh. For the next few verses (18:4-9) Abraham regards the three men as ordinary travelers, but when the birth of a son is announced (18:10-14), the spokesman for the group turns out to be "the LORD." In verse 22 the men who depart toward Sodom are probably two of the visitors, since Abraham is left standing "before the LORD." In 19:1 the two angels ("the men" of chapter 18?) arrive at Sodom, but in 19:21-22 again the Lord seems to be speaking. Perhaps the best way to explain these variations in the story is to assume that Yahweh is repre- sented in the three heavenly visitors. By this imprecision the writer is obviously trying to conceal the true identity of Yahweh.

The three visitors accept Abraham's gracious hospitality and partake of a sumptuous bedouin meal which he prepares for them, consisting of bread, made in the form of large, flat discs, tender meat of a calf, and two kinds of milk—curdled, or leban, as it is known among the Arabs today, and fresh. According to Near Eastern custom, Sarah does not appear before the male visitors, and Abraham, as the host, stands by while his guests eat, to see that they get every attention. After the meal the vis- itors get down to the business of the day. They bring the start- ling news to Abraham that Sarah, his wife, who is advanced in years, is going to have a son by the next year (see also 17:21). When Sarah, who is eavesdropping at the tent door, hears these words, she laughs and says, "After I have grown old, and my hus- band is old, shall I have pleasure?" (18:12). Her incredulous laughter, like that of Abraham (17:17), explains the name of Isaac ("he laughs"), the son of promise. In response to Sarah's skepticism the Lord says, "Is anything too hard for the LORD?" (18:14). Obviously, there is nothing too difficult or too wonderful (both meanings are associated with the Hebrew word found in this verse) for God to do (see Luke 1:37). He who created the heavens and the earth and all their host is able to do all things. He can even accomplish his divine purpose by things which are not (I Cor. 1:28).

Abraham Intercedes for Sodom (18:16-33) [J]

Abraham, the courteous host, accompanies his guests for part of the way on the road toward Sodom, their ultimate destination. "So the men turned from there, and went toward Sodom; but Abraham still stood before the LORD" (18:22). Before Abraham makes his impassioned plea for Sodom, the writer injects a brief but interesting passage in which Yahweh debates with himself whether he should tell Abraham about the imminent doom of Sodom (18:17-19). He decides to do so because of his special relation to Abraham. He has chosen Abraham to establish the true faith among men and to be the recipient of the divine promise. He will now draw the veil and allow Abraham to behold the mysterious workings of divine judgment so that he may teach his children to shun evil and walk in the ways of righteousness and justice (see II Peter 2:6-10).

Aware of the impending destruction of Sodom, Abraham boldly approaches the Lord to intercede for the city. "Wilt thou indeed destroy the righteous with the wicked?" is the question that Abraham asks (18:23). Although Abraham is no doubt deeply concerned about Lot and his family who live in the city, he is mainly interested in the larger issue of God's justice as it relates to the destruction of the whole city. With his keen sense of justice and his genuine love for mankind, Abraham cannot believe that God, "the Judge of all the earth" (18:25), will destroy the righteous with the wicked. Therefore, even though he recognizes that he is but "dust and ashes" (18:27) in the sight of God, he pleads with God to spare Sodom if he finds fifty righteous people in it. When God agrees to spare Sodom for the sake of fifty righteous, Abraham grows more bold and asks for Sodom's deliverance if only forty-five righteous are found. To this God also agrees. So the bargaining goes on until God is willing to spare the city for the sake of ten righteous. "And the LORD went his way, when he had finished speaking to Abraham; and Abraham returned to his place" (18:33).

Several things impress us as we read this amazing story of intercession. First, there is the concern of this complete stranger for the wicked citizens of Sodom. Why should a wandering nomad imperil his life for these people in warfare (chapter 14), and then plead so earnestly with God for their deliverance? Abraham's love for his fellow men springs from his love for God. He who is "the friend of God" (James 2:23) embraces all men in his compassion. Then, too, Abraham's persistent pleading for Sodom reveals an unshakable faith in the ultimate justice and goodness of God. As Abraham's mathematics decreased from fifty to ten, his faith increased inversely. Therefore, "God remembered Abraham, and sent Lot out of the midst of the overthrow, when he overthrew the cities" (19:29).

Lastly, we see in this story the preservative power of a few righteous people. For the sake of ten good persons God will not destroy Sodom, and, according to 19:22, he will not overthrow the city until Lot leaves. God's mercy is supreme, and the righteous one is saved. "You are the salt of the earth," Jesus said; "but if salt has lost its taste, how shall its saltness be restored? It is no longer good for anything except to be thrown out and trodden under foot by men" (Matt. 5:13). By the presence of God-fearing people in the world, the overwhelming power of evil is restrained and the wrath of God is turned back.

The Destruction of Sodom (19:1-38) [J]

The two angels—probably the "men" who had taken their leave of Abraham in 18:22—arrive in Sodom in the evening and are cordially welcomed into the home of Lot. The house is soon surrounded by the men of Sodom, clamoring for the guests inside. Lot, who is obligated to protect the visitors who have found shelter under his roof, offers his daughters to the perverted assailants, but they refuse to have them, and threaten to molest Lot, who is reminded of his solitary, defenseless state in the city of Sodom. (See also the account of the ravishing of the Levite's concubine by the men of Gibeah in Judges 19.) Lot is saved from the rabble by his two guests, who pull him back into the house and strike the men at the door with blindness. After this repulsive scene the guests reveal to Lot the purpose of their mission. They tell him that Sodom is doomed because of the sin of the people and that he and his family should get out as soon as possible. "Flee for your life; do not look back or stop anywhere in the valley; flee to the hills, lest you be consumed" (19:17). Although Lot, his wife, and his two daughters are somewhat reluctant, they are led from the city by the visitors, the Lord being merciful to them (19:16). "But Lot's wife behind him looked back, and she became a pillar of salt" (19:26). Her backward glance revealed that her heart was still in Sodom, and that she was loath to give up the joys and pleasures of this world in obedience to God's command. "Remember Lot's wife," Jesus said. "Whoever seeks to gain his life will lose it, but whoever loses his life will preserve it" (Luke 17:32-33).

The destruction of Sodom and Gomorrah was probably due to earthquake activity, as the terms "overthrew" and "overthrow" (19:25, 29) seem to indicate. The fissures in the earth destroyed the cities and released sulphurous gases (brimstone) and seepages of asphalt (bitumen) which became ignited and caused a great holocaust (19:28). Archaeological evidence indicates that the Cities of the Plain, including Sodom and Gomorrah (see 14:2), lie submerged under the rather shallow water of the southern part of the Dead Sea. This catastrophe is frequently referred to in later books of the Bible (Deut. 29:23; Jer. 20:16; Amos 4:11; Luke 17:29; II Peter 2:6).

The rather indelicate story of the birth of Moab and Ammon to the daughters of Lot (19:30-38), which brings the chapter to a close, explains the origin of the Moabites and Ammonites and their close relation to the Israelites. The account of the incestuous birth of the progenitors of these nations probably reflects the feelings of contempt and hatred that Israel had for their neighbors across the Jordan (see Deut. 23:3). The statement of Lot's elder daughter that "there is not a man on earth to come in to us after the manner of all the earth" (19:31) indicates her conviction that the existence of the race is at stake. Many ancient marital customs—for example, levirate marriage, when a kinsman takes the widow of his deceased brother to wife; polygamy; taking a slave to wife, as Abraham and Hagar; and even incest in extreme cases as here, which later generations frown upon—must be understood in the light of man's struggle for survival in the face of a hostile world.

Abraham and Sarah in Gerar (20:1-18) [E]

The story of Abraham, Sarah, and Abimelech in this chapter is very similar to the episode of Abraham's sojourn in Egypt where Sarah was taken into the house of Pharaoh (12:10-20). "From there" (20:1) is ambiguous, unless it means that Abraham had left the region of Hebron from which he had viewed the terrible destruction of Sodom (19:27-28). He wanders southward through the Negeb until he comes to Gerar, a site near Gaza, where he sojourns. In remarkably few words we are told that Sarah is Abraham's sister (20:12; compare 12:13, 19), and that Abimelech, the king of Gerar, took her into his harem (20:2). "But God came to Abimelech in a dream by night, and said to him, 'Behold, you are a dead man, because of the woman whom you have taken; for she is a man's wife'" (20:3). It is rather remarkable that God should appear to a foreign ruler in a dream and hold a conversation with him. After Abimelech protests his innocence in this whole matter, since Abraham had not told him that Sarah was his wife, God says to him in a dream, "Yes, I know that you have done this in the integrity of your heart, and it was I who kept you from sinning against me; therefore I did not let you touch her. Now then restore the man's wife; for he is a prophet, and he will pray for you, and you shall live. But if you do not restore her, know that you shall surely die, you, and all that are yours" (20:6-7). From this divine revelation we learn that the king had not yet come near Sarah, probably because of some kind of sickness that God brought upon the household (see 20:17), and so he was mercifully prevented from sinning against God.

The strong denunciation of adultery in this story as a sin against God shows a high standard of ethics. We also note that Abraham is called a "prophet." The word is found here for the first time in the Bible. As used here, it means a man who, because of his close relationship with God, can intercede efficaciously for his fellow men (see also Amos 3:7; Jer. 7:16). Abimelech, who is frightened because of the dream he had in the night, calls Abraham to him and rebukes him for allowing him to do "things that ought not to be done" (20:9). Abraham, in self-defense, gives three excuses. First, he was afraid for his life. "I did it because I thought, There is no fear of God at all in this place, and they will kill me because of my wife" (20:11).

He is completely at the mercy of pagan people who could take his life without any fear of divine retribution. Secondly, he claims that he was not lying when he said that Sarah was his sister, for she actually was the daughter of his father, but not of his mother (20:12). And thirdly, Abraham reveals that he had schemed with Sarah that she should refer to herself as his sister at the time he set out from his father's house (20:13).

Abimelech is evidently satisfied with these explanations and gives Abraham presents as compensation for the injury unwittingly done to his honor. He also invites him to remain in his land and dwell wheresoever he wishes (see also 12:19-20). And to Sarah, Abimelech said, "Behold, I have given your brother [note the sarcasm] a thousand pieces of silver; it is your vindication in the eyes of all who are with you; and before every one you are righted" (20:16). Thus Sarah's character is completely vindicated before her family and all men. After Abimelech treats his honored guests in this lavish way, Abraham prays to God (20:17) and God removes the barrenness which had fallen as a divine judgment upon the royal household.

The Birth of Isaac (21:1-7) [J, E, P]

Isaac is born to Sarah as the Lord had promised (17:19). The old age of Sarah and Abraham at the time of Isaac's birth is again noted (21:2, 7; see also 18:11; 24:36). The naming of the child and his circumcision when eight days old are in accordance with 17:19, 12. The name Isaac, which comes from a Hebrew root meaning "to laugh," was originally part of a full sentence in which the name of the Deity appeared as the subject. It meant, "may the deity laugh [over] the child." Other names which have the same sentence pattern are Ishmael, Jacob, and Israel. In 21:6 there is a combination of two different traditions regarding the meaning of the name Isaac. In one, he is so called because Sarah rejoices over the fact that God has made her fruitful; according to the other, the friends of Sarah will laugh when they hear the news that she has borne a son.

The Expulsion of Ishmael (21:8-21) [E]

The time of weaning a child, which occurs in Eastern lands anywhere from two to four years after birth, is celebrated by a joyous family feast. It is on this occasion that "Sarah saw the son of Hagar the Egyptian, whom she had borne to Abraham,

playing with her son Isaac" (21:9). This writer (E) evidently
thinks of Ishmael here as quite a young child (see also 21:15)
playing with the infant Isaac, although according to 16:16 and
21:5 (P) Ishmael must have been about seventeen years old
by this time. The root of the verb translated "playing" is the
one from which the name "Isaac" is derived. The later fanciful
interpretations of this word in Jewish circles are reflected in
Paul's allusion to Ishmael's persecuting Isaac (Gal. 4:29).
Sarah's jealousy is aroused as she sees her son playing with the
child of her handmaid, and so she demands that Abraham cast
the slave woman and her son out of the house. As we learn in the
recently discovered Nuzu documents, however, it was not legal to
expel the handmaid and her offspring after the wife had a child
of her own. It is for this reason, no doubt, that Abraham is reluctant to comply with Sarah's request (21:11), and it is only because of a special word from God himself that Abraham finally
sends Hagar and Ishmael forth (21:12-13).

Hagar and Ishmael wander in the wilderness of Beer-sheba
until their meager provisions are exhausted. Racked with thirst,
she casts her child under a bush and sits down a bowshot away
so that she will not see him die. According to the last two verbs
in the Hebrew text of 21:16, Hagar "lifted up her voice and
wept." A much more effective picture of Hagar's tearless despair is given in the Greek translation of this passage, followed
by the English, which reads, "the child lifted up his voice and
wept." Divine care and mercy for those who are outside the
special Covenant relation is shown here in two ways. First, "the
angel of God," who speaks from heaven, informs Hagar that
God has heard the child's cry, and that she should arise and
take the child's hand, for "I will make him a great nation"
(21:18; see 21:13; 25:12-18). And secondly, Hagar's eyes are
opened so that she sees a well of water nearby from which she
and her child may drink. Ishmael grows up under divine protection and dwells in the desert between Egypt and Canaan,
where he becomes an expert bowman. His mother selects his
wife from Egypt, her own native land. Ishmael's history is
shown here to be a parallel to "holy history," blessed by God
but not a part of the Covenant seed. This is another testing of
Abraham's faith, for by sending Ishmael away he has to give
up a son whom he dearly loves. His hopes are now centered

more than ever on Isaac, which makes the trial of the following chapter particularly severe for Abraham.

The Covenant Between Abimelech and Abraham (21:22-34) [E, J]

There are two stories intertwined in this section, both of which explain the origin of the place name Beer-sheba. In the first account (21:22-24, 27, 31) Abimelech desires to make a treaty with Abraham, seeing that God is with him in all that he does. "Now therefore swear to me here by God that you will not deal falsely with me or with my offspring or with my posterity, but as I have dealt loyally with you, you will deal with me and with the land where you have sojourned" (21:23). To this Abraham agrees, and a covenant is established between the two men (21:27). Beer-sheba, which means "well of oath," thus derives its name from the fact that Abimelech and Abraham "swore an oath" at this place (21:31).

Behind this account of the establishment of friendly relations between Abimelech and Abraham, however, one detects the rumblings of a serious dispute over the possession of a well which Abraham and his men had dug in the desert. This is the subject of the second stratum of this section (21:25-26, 28-30, 32). Evidently the servants of Abimelech had seized a well from Abraham and his men, and when Abraham complains, Abimelech disclaims any knowledge of his men's actions. In a land where water is scarce, disputes like this over the possession of wells were a common occurrence (see 26:20-33). The argument is finally settled when Abraham gives Abimelech seven ewe lambs. By stressing the number "seven" in verses 28-30 the writer is apparently trying to explain the etymology of the name Beer-sheba as "well of seven," or "seven wells," referring to the number of wells in the vicinity. Since the root of the Hebrew verb "to swear" (literally, "to seven oneself") and the word for "seven" are closely related, the two etymologies of Beer-sheba suggested here are practically identical. After the claim of Abraham to this site is recognized by Abimelech, the patriarch plants a tree which marks Beer-sheba as a religious site for generations to come (see Amos 5:5; 8:14). The mention of the "land of the Philistines" (21:32; see also 26:1) as the place where Abimelech lived must be regarded as an anachronism, since we know from the implications of biblical history and from archaeological evidence that the Philistines did not settle in this region until after 1200 B.C.

The Sacrifice of Isaac (22:1-19) [E], (22:20-24) [J]

Here is the supreme test of Abraham's faith. After Abraham
had left his homeland in response to the divine call, and had
received the promise of an heir and the land of Canaan as his
inheritance, his faith was sorely tested by many trials and disappointments. Of these the most severe is the one described in the
passage before us. Abraham is now ordered by God to take
Isaac, the son of promise, the child whom he loved, to the land
of Moriah, the exact location of which is not known, and offer
him up there as a sacrifice on one of the mountains which God
will show him. He who had said, "Through Isaac shall your
descendants be named" (21:12), now says, "Take your son . . .
and offer him there as a burnt offering" (22:2). God seems to
be contradicting himself. He is asking Abraham to give back
the son whom he had received as a miraculous gift from the
very beginning. The one who was born to bring salvation to the
world is thus to be taken out of history. Such a prospect is beyond all human reason and comprehension.

The problem here is one of obedience to God's word in the
face of utter despair and hopelessness. Can Abraham accept
the fact that Isaac is not his own, but a pure gift of God's
grace whom God had given and can take away at his pleasure?
The answer is not long in coming. "So Abraham rose early in
the morning . . . On the third day Abraham lifted up his eyes
and saw the place afar off" (22:3-4). The determination of
Abraham to obey God's command is clearly marked in these
two statements, although not a word is spoken about his anguish
of soul as he marches with his son toward the place of sacrifice.
So far as Abraham is concerned, Isaac is dead. God has commanded him to slay Isaac, and that he will do. There is no
middle course between life and death. And what about the
promises of seed and land which God had made to Abraham?
Abraham had come to know that God was true to his word.
Isaac himself is the living witness to the fact that God's promises
are sure and true. How could this contradiction of the death of
Isaac and the fulfillment of the promise be resolved? By clinging
to the promise, Abraham can only believe that God, in his own
way and by his own wisdom, will raise seed to Isaac, even
though he is dead. Already he has seen how God had made the
barren womb of Sarah fruitful. Why could he not also even raise

Isaac from the dead? "Is anything too wonderful for the LORD?" (18:14, margin).

His faith strengthened by this new insight into the mercy and power of God, Abraham prepares the altar for the sacrifice of Isaac and is ready to slay him, when the Angel of the Lord stays his hand and prevents the fatal act. Abraham sees a ram caught in a nearby thicket and offers it up as a sacrifice in place of his son. Thus Isaac, who was as good as dead, is restored to his father (see Heb. 11:19). The hope of Abraham that God would provide a lamb for the offering (vs. 8) is now realized, "So Abraham called the name of that place The LORD will provide" (22:14). As a reward for Abraham's obedience, the Lord, through his messenger, renews the promises of numerous seed and the inheritance of the land (22:16-18; compare 12:1-3, 7; 13:14-17; 15:7, 18; 17:4-8), and adds a new note, that his descendants shall conquer and possess the cities of the land (22:17). The chapter closes with a genealogy of Nahor, Abraham's brother, who lived in Haran in northern Syria (22:20-24). These closing verses set the stage for the story in chapter 24, where Abraham's servant returns to the old homestead in Haran and brings back Rebekah as a wife for Isaac.

The Purchase of the Cave of Machpelah (23:1-20) [P]

Sarah, the wife of Abraham, dies in Hebron at the age of one hundred and twenty-seven years. Perhaps there is some connection between her death and the terrible ordeal suffered by her son Isaac, described in the preceding chapter. Abraham, who is still a stranger and sojourner in the land, resolves to buy a piece of property in which he may bury his wife. He negotiates with the Hittites, one of the groups of people in Canaan at this time, who offer him their choicest of sepulchres as a gift. This Abraham refuses to accept, insisting instead on paying for a piece of ground where he may bury his dead. With typical oriental courtesy, Ephron, the Hittite, offers Abraham a piece of land worth four hundred shekels of silver, but "what is that between you and me?" he slyly asks (23:15). Abraham takes the hint and pays out four hundred shekels for the land. "So the field of Ephron in Machpelah, which was to the east of Mamre, the field with the cave which was in it and all the trees that were in the field, throughout its whole area, was made over to Abraham as a possession in the presence of the Hittites, be-

fore all who went in at the gate of his city [that is, before those
who have a voice in the affairs of the community]" (23:17-18).
Thus the only land that Abraham ever comes to own in Canaan
is a burial plot. He inherits the Promised Land only in death.
Sarah is laid to rest in the cave of Machpelah, where later Abraham (25:9), Isaac (35:29), Rebekah and Leah (49:31), and
Jacob (50:13) are to be buried. Today the traditional site of the
cave in Hebron is covered by a large mosque. Here through the
centuries Muslim, Christian, and Jew have honored Abraham,
revered in the three great monotheistic religions of the world.

The Story of Isaac and Rebekah (24:1-67) [J]

Abraham has one last duty to perform—to find a wife for
his son Isaac, the heir of the promise. This is a most important
task, for the wife of Isaac will be the one through whom the
divine blessing given to Abraham will be passed on to future
generations. It is therefore imperative that the right wife be
found for Isaac. This quest is the subject of the longest chapter
in the Book of Genesis. It is one of the most beautiful stories in
all the patriarchal narratives, marked by simplicity and clarity
of style, and giving one of the most vivid pictures of ancient
oriental life to be found in the Old Testament. Abraham calls
his oldest and most trustworthy servant—probably Eliezer of
Damascus, mentioned in 15:2—and makes him swear, first
that he will not take a wife from the Canaanites for Isaac; second, that he will go to Haran, the city of Nahor, to get a wife
for Isaac; and third, that he will never take Isaac back to his
relatives in Syria. If, however, the young maiden is unwilling
to come to Canaan and marry Isaac, then the servant will be
free of the oath which he has sworn.

By ordering his servant to carry out these strict orders under
oath, Abraham is safeguarding the divine promises which were
made to him when he entered Canaan. Marriage with the
Canaanites is forbidden, not only to preserve the purity of the
stock, but to avoid contamination with the immoral practices
of the Canaanite religion. And Isaac could not go back to Haran
to marry and settle down since that would mean rejection of the
way of salvation as God had planned it. The fact that Abraham
makes his servant swear an oath (24:2-9) may indicate that the
patriarch believes his death is imminent. To emphasize the sanctity of the oath, the servant puts his hand under Abraham's thigh

(see 47:29, where Joseph's pledge to the dying Jacob is solemnized in the same way). The significance of this ancient rite is no longer clear. Perhaps the touching of the thigh, which is a euphemistic term for the organs of generation, is a symbolic way of indicating that a man's descendants are being invoked to uphold the oath, or avenge any infraction thereof.

The detailed account of the servant's journey, his meeting with the young maiden at the well outside the city of Nahor, her kind and gracious response to his request for water, and his warm reception at the old homestead indicate that nothing is unimportant on a divinely appointed mission like this. God's overruling providence is seen in every detail. The servant's prayer that the Lord will prosper his way (24:12-14) is answered, for the young maiden he meets at the well is Rebekah, the daughter of Bethuel, Abraham's nephew (24:24; see 22:20, 23) and brother of Laban. In 24:30-32 the avaricious character of Laban, more fully displayed in his contacts with Jacob (especially chs. 29-30), is already hinted at.

After Rebekah consents to accompany the servant, the caravan sets out for Canaan. When they come as far as the Negeb, they see Isaac who had gone out "to meditate in the field in the evening" (24:63). Rebekah alights from her camel (literally, "fell off," but see II Kings 5:21, where the same verb is used for alighting from a chariot), and veils herself, according to oriental custom, before her betrothed. After Isaac is told all the things that had happened on the journey, he takes Rebekah for his wife and he is comforted after his mother's death. The theological motif of this chapter, like that of the Joseph story, is that God will lead and prosper the one who puts his trust in him. It is expressed in the words of the servant, "the LORD has prospered my way" (24:56; see also vss. 21, 40, 42).

The Death of Abraham; Genealogies (25:1-18) [J, P]

Abraham takes another wife—presumably after the death of Sarah—by the name of Keturah. Through her Abraham becomes the ancestor of numerous Arab tribes (25:1-4). He gives gifts to the sons of his concubines and sends them away "eastward to the east country" (25:6). Isaac alone remains in Canaan, and as the only rightful heir he receives all that Abraham has, excepting, of course, the gifts mentioned above (25:5).

Then Abraham dies at the good old age of one hundred and

seventy-five years. He is buried by Isaac and Ishmael in the cave of Machpelah beside Sarah his wife (25:7-11). The story of Ishmael's expulsion (ch. 21) is ignored. Or perhaps Isaac and Ishmael were reconciled at the grave of their father.

The genealogy of Ishmael is now given, before the history of the Chosen People is resumed (25:12-18). In fulfillment of Genesis 17:20, twelve sons are born to Ishmael and become the leaders or "princes" (25:15) of their respective tribes. The death of Ishmael at one hundred and thirty-seven years of age is also recorded (25:17). The descendants of Ishmael were, for the most part, bedouins who lived in the desert region of northeast Arabia.

The Jacob Story (25:19—36:43)

The Birth of Esau and Jacob (25:19-26) [P, J]

Isaac's birth and marriage, more fully described before in 21:1-3 and chapter 24, are again mentioned here (25:19-20) as a fitting introduction to his "generations." "And Isaac prayed to the LORD for his wife, because she was barren; and the LORD granted his prayer, and Rebekah his wife conceived" (25:21). Once again we are reminded that the line of descent in the special history of salvation depends entirely upon the grace of God. Isaac, Jacob, and Joseph (29:31; 30:22-24) are all children of miraculous birth. Salvation is entirely the activity of God, "so that no human being might boast in the presence of God" (I Cor. 1:29). Rebekah inquires of the Lord regarding the children who are struggling together in her womb, and she receives an answer in the form of a poetic oracle, which states that the two children in her womb are two nations, that their struggling prefigures future rivalries between the two nations, and that the younger will prevail over the older. These prophetic words refer, of course, to the birth of Esau and Jacob, the ancestors, respectively, of Edom and Israel; to the hostility which existed between these peoples down through the centuries; and to the favored position of Israel above Edom in God's plan of redemption. Why God should "love" Jacob and "hate" Esau (Mal. 1:2-3), or why God should elect Jacob and not Esau, even before they were born (Rom. 9:10-13), is not for us to question. God calls whom he will, irrespective of class, color, race, or rank. The twins are named from the circumstances of birth. "The first came forth

red, all his body like a hairy mantle; so they called his name
Esau" (25:25). Actually there are two etymologies here, or,
more accurately, two puns. The Hebrew word for "red" is a play
on the name Edom (see vs. 30), and the Hebrew word for
"hairy" is a play on the name Seir (see 33:16), the home of
Esau's descendants. The meaning of the name Esau is not certain.
The description of Esau as dark and hairy reveals the deep-seated
contempt Israel had for her neighbor. The name Jacob, which is
popularly associated with the Hebrew word for "heel," is derived
from the fact that when he was born, "his hand had taken hold of
Esau's heel" (25:26), as though even in the womb he were trying
to get ahead of Esau and be born first. The original meaning of
Jacob, "may God protect," seems to have been forgotten.

Esau Sells His Birthright (25:27-34) [J]

The two boys grow up to be men of different temperaments,
each one choosing a distinctive way of life. Esau becomes a skillful hunter, who loves the out-of-doors. He is the favorite of his
father because he brings him game from the field. Jacob, on the
other hand, lives the more sedentary life of the herdsman, which
was the patriarchal ideal. He is the favorite of his mother. Esau,
the hunter, whose existence at best is a precarious one, is hungry
one day after the chase. He notices that Jacob, the shepherd,
who always has food, is "boiling something that is boiling," as
the Hebrew has it (25:29a). He is famished, and says to Jacob,
"Let me gulp some of the red—that red there!" Jacob, taking advantage of Esau's exhausted condition, offers him the food on
condition that he sell him his birthright. Esau, about to die, as he
says, sees little value in his birthright at the moment, and so he
sells it to Jacob for some bread and boiled lentils. The statement
that "Esau despised his birthright" (25:34) is the only word of
judgment in the story. A later writer condemns Esau more severely, when he calls him "immoral or irreligious" because he
sold his birthright for a single meal (Heb. 12:16).

The significance of this event for the understanding of the
Christmas story as recorded in the second chapter of Matthew is
often overlooked. The reason that Herod "was troubled" (Matt.
2:3) when he heard about the birth of a King of the Jews arose
from the fact that Herod was an Idumean, that is, an Edomite,
or descendant of Esau (Gen. 25:30). He knew that he was a
foreigner and usurper, and, as a descendant of Esau, had no

right to be ruler over the descendants of Jacob (Israel). The situation of the elder serving the younger—that is, of Esau serving Jacob, as prophesied in the oracle to Rebekah (Gen. 25:23) and actualized in the sale of Esau's birthright to Jacob—was completely reversed at the time of Jesus' birth. It was for this reason that Herod, moved with jealous rage, commanded that all male children, two years or under, in Bethlehem and the surrounding region, should be slain. By issuing this terrible command, Herod undoubtedly believed he was destroying the rightful King of the Jews who was to come of the line of Jacob (Israel).

Incidents in the Life of Isaac (26:1-35) [J, P]

This chapter is the only one that contains stories in which Isaac plays the leading role. In other places in the patriarchal tradition he is mentioned in connection either with his father, Abraham, or with his sons, Jacob and Esau. Isaac is the least spectacular of the patriarchs, yet, as the son of an illustrious father and the father of an illustrious son, he is a vital link in the chain of the history of salvation. The tradition concerning Isaac preserved in this chapter is a mosaic of six different episodes in his life (26:1-6, 7-11, 12-17, 18-22, 23-25, 26-33), to which has been attached (vss. 34-35) a notice of Esau's Hittite wives. The first four of these episodes occur in Gerar, and the last two in Beer-sheba, both places being located in southern Palestine. We shall discuss these incidents in the order in which they appear in the chapter.

Isaac, who dwelt at Beer-lahai-roi (25:11) near Kadesh-Barnea, is forced to move with his family and flocks because of a famine. Instead of going to Egypt, which was the usual place of asylum at a time like this (see the Joseph story), Isaac goes "to Gerar, to Abimelech king of the Philistines," where God appears to him in some kind of manifestation and advises him to remain, pronouncing upon him the patriarchal blessing of numerous seed and inheritance of the land of promise. According to this statement of the promise, Isaac receives the blessing "because Abraham obeyed my voice and kept my charge, my commandments, my statutes, and my laws" (26:5). So Isaac dwells in Gerar. The Abimelech of these episodes is probably not the Abimelech of the Abraham story (chs. 20 and 21), since there is a lapse of some eighty years between the two events. The reference to Abimelech as "king of the Philistines" is again anachronistic, as has been noted before, since the Philistines did not arrive in the southwestern part of Palestine until sometime after 1200 B.C.

Isaac, fearing that the men of Gerar would kill him because of Rebekah his wife, tells them that she is his sister. The similarity of this story to those of Abraham and Sarah in Egypt (12: 1-20) and in Gerar (ch. 20) is obvious. Many students believe that in these three accounts we have three slightly different versions of the same basic incident. In the stories of Abraham and Sarah there was some basis for Abraham's passing Sarah off as his sister, since she was "the daughter of my father but not the daughter of my mother" (20:12); but Isaac could in no way claim that Rebekah was his sister. After Abimelech finds out that Rebekah is really Isaac's wife he rebukes him for his deceit, and warns all the people, saying, "Whoever touches this man or his wife shall be put to death" (26:11). In this story, as in the other two similar accounts, we are reminded of the moral weakness of the patriarchs, and of God's care for his own among strange people and in dangerous circumstances.

Isaac's phenomenal success as a farmer in the region of Gerar leads the Philistines to regard him with envy. To show their displeasure they fill with earth the wells which Abraham's servants had dug, thus making it impossible for Isaac to sojourn in the land. At Abimelech's suggestion, Isaac departs from the town of Gerar and dwells in the valley of Gerar.

In the valley of Gerar, Isaac digs two wells, called Esek and Sitnah. These are contested by the herdsman of Gerar, and so he moves on and makes another well whose name he calls Rehoboth, which literally means "wide places." Prosperity is now assured Isaac since he has unhindered access to a supply of water.

The last two incidents in this cycle of stories take place in Beer-sheba. According to this passage the Lord appears to Isaac at Beer-sheba and blesses him "for my servant Abraham's sake." This is the only place in Genesis where Abraham is referred to as "my servant." In connection with this manifestation of God, Isaac builds an altar at Beer-sheba and calls on the name of the Lord. He also pitches his tent there and his servants dig a well. Israel long remembered this ancient tradition which linked Isaac with Beer-sheba as a religious site (see also 46:1).

Abimelech, who sees that Isaac's prosperity can be explained only as the result of God's blessing, thinks it best to come to terms with such a powerful man. He suggests that they make a covenant, and he dictates the terms: ". . . you will do us no harm, just as we have not touched you and have done to you nothing but good and have sent you away in peace" (26:29). They eat the covenant meal (see 31:54), and swear an oath to keep the agreement. On the same day Isaac learns that the well which his men have dug is producing water. Once again we have the setting for the naming of Beer-sheba, "the well of oath" (see 21:22-32).

To the Isaac tradition has been appended the notice of Esau's marriage to two Hittite women. This intermarriage with members of the people of the land is a source of great sorrow and worry to the parents of Esau.

Jacob Defrauds Esau of His Blessing (27:1-45) [J, E]

Isaac is now old and his eyes are dim, and he feels it is time to give his blessing to his oldest son, Esau, before he dies. He asks Esau to prepare for him his favorite dish of food from the chase, not simply because he is especially fond of it, but in order to strengthen himself so that his "soul power" may go forth from him in the blessing. The last words of a dying man were considered to be especially potent and to have prophetic significance. They were irrevocable when once spoken, and, according to recent evidence from Nuzu, they were also legally binding.

In verses 5-17 we learn about Rebekah's strategem to secure the patriarchal blessing, which rightly belonged to Esau, the first-born, for her favorite son, Jacob, the younger brother. Like Sarah (18:10), Rebekah is eavesdropping when Isaac tells Esau that he wants to bless him. Quickly and expertly she devises a plan whereby she hopes to deceive Isaac and secure the blessing for Jacob. She prepares a savory meal for Isaac, dresses Jacob in Esau's festal clothes, and covers his hands and neck with the skins of kids, since Esau was a hairy man (see 25:25), and sends him in to Isaac with the food she has prepared.

It is now up to Jacob himself to carry out the daring plan successfully (vss. 18-29). The tension of the reader mounts as Jacob faces Isaac. Will the ruse be discovered? Will Jacob be recognized by the aged father? In answer to Isaac's first question, "Who are you, my son?" Jacob deliberately lies and tells him that he is Esau. When Isaac's suspicions are further aroused by the rapidity with which the game was caught and the meal prepared, Jacob blasphemously answers, "The LORD your God granted me success." Still not satisfied, Isaac asks Jacob to come near that he may feel him. The tension is almost unbearable.

This is the supreme test, the moment that Jacob had dreaded when his mother unfolded her contemptible plan before him. But her ruse is successful, for "he did not recognize him, because his hands were hairy like his brother Esau's hands; so he blessed him" (27:23), the last words anticipating verses 27-29. Isaac eats the food that Jacob brought and prepares to bless him. " 'Come near and kiss me, my son.' So he came near and kissed him; and he smelled the smell of his garments, and blessed him" (27:26-27). The smell of the field on Jacob's raiment dispels from Isaac's mind the last shadow of doubt of his son's identity and suggests the opening words of the blessing which follows. The odor of the Holy Land, with its rich agricultural resources, shall cling to Jacob (Israel) forever, and nations far and near shall bow before him in recognition of his power and prestige.

Now follows one of the most pitiable scenes in all literature (27:30-40). Esau, returning from the hunt, prepares his father's favorite dish and brings it to him, awaiting the paternal blessing. When Isaac realizes what he has done, he trembles with terror (literally in Hebrew, "he trembled with an exceedingly great trembling"). He cannot retract the words of blessing which he has pronounced upon Jacob, for, according to Hebrew psychology, the word, once spoken, goes forth like a missile to accomplish its purpose—blessing or curse—and can never be taken back (see Isa. 55:11). On learning what had happened, Esau "cried out with an exceedingly great and bitter cry, and said to his father, 'Bless me, even me also, O my father!' " (27:34). The blessing which he has foolishly squandered for bread and lentils once again eludes him. "Is he not rightly named Jacob? For he has supplanted me these two times," cries Esau. Yet all the tears of bitterness and frustration cannot regain for Esau the privileges which he has so foolishly forfeited (see Heb. 12:17). Although Esau realizes that the blessing given to Jacob cannot be recalled, he asks his father if he does not have even one blessing for him. Isaac replies with a poetic oracle which is actually more of a curse than a blessing. Esau's dwelling will be far from the rich fields of the earth and the dew of heaven. The land of Edom is indeed bleak and barren in comparison with the land of Canaan. Edom shall live by the sword, raiding and plundering her neighbors and the caravans which pass across her borders. Edom is doomed to subjection under Israel, but there will be times when Edom will break the yoke of his

brother (see II Kings 8:20-22; 16:6). There is little in these
words of blessing from Isaac to soothe the bitterness in Esau's
heart. When Rebekah learns that Esau is planning to kill Jacob
after Isaac dies, she advises Jacob to leave home for his health
and visit her brother Laban in Haran for "a few days" (so literally in 27:44), until the whole affair is forgotten. The "few
days" turns out to be more than twenty years (see 31:41).
Rebekah presumably never sees her favorite son again, since
she probably dies while he is in Haran.

We may well ask ourselves, What is the value of this story?
What purpose does it serve in the Bible? It would appear from
the events recorded in this chapter that deception is condoned
as a means for gaining one's end, and there are those who see
no moral value in the story at all. It is, in fact, hard to understand anyone who would plan the deception of a blind old man,
or who would not be moved by the anguished cries of a brother
who has just lost his most treasured possession. We may not be
able to explain the motives of a Rebekah, or the brazen audacity
of a Jacob, but what the writer is interested in showing is that
God's redemptive purpose for the ultimate salvation of the
world is advanced even through the sinister connivings of a
Rebekah and a Jacob. Jacob received the blessing, which is the
important point of the story, and it could not be taken back.
The personal relations of the members of Isaac's family are
overshadowed by the divine purpose and plan.

Jacob's Dream at Bethel (27:46—28:22) [P, J, E]

In 27:46—28:9 we have another tradition (P) of Jacob's
blessing and his journey to Syria. Rebekah's mention of Hittite
women in 27:46 connects the passage with 26:34-35 (P) where
Esau is said to have married two Hittite girls. The reason in this
passage for sending Jacob to Paddan-aram (Syria, or the Aramean country), therefore, is to avoid intermarriage with "the
women of the land" (27:46). According to this account Isaac
sends Jacob to Laban after blessing him, and the story of Jacob's
deception is not mentioned. Neither is anything said about
Esau's resentment, or Jacob's secret, hurried flight to Haran to
escape the wrath of his brother. Hosea, the prophet, follows the
older tradition of J (27:41-45) when he says, "Jacob fled to the
land of Aram" (Hosea 12:12). Esau, according to the P account
(28:6-9), desirous of a blessing from Isaac, follows Jacob's exam-

ple, and marries his cousin, Mahalath, the daughter of Ishmael.

The story of Jacob's dream at Bethel follows (28:10-22). On the way from Beer-sheba to Haran, Jacob comes upon "a certain place" (literally, "the place," as though well-known [see 12:6 and 8], later identified as Bethel, vs. 19) where he decides to spend the night. He lays his head upon a stone—it would be hard to find a place at Bethel where there is no stone—and goes to sleep. During the night he dreams a dream. "There was a ladder set up on the earth, and the top of it reached to heaven; and behold, the angels of God were ascending and descending on it!" (28:12). By "ladder" in this verse we must not understand an ordinary stepladder with wooden rungs; the Hebrew word, which basically means a "piling up," suggests a sloping ascent, and so may refer to the steplike structures found in the Mesopotamian Valley, known as ziggurats (see 11:4), with a temple on top to which man ascended in his worship of the deity. The stairs which Jacob sees unite heaven and earth, and the messengers of God are ascending and descending upon them. Like the angelic patrols in Zechariah's first vision (Zech. 1:8-11), the messengers of God go throughout the world, carrying out his orders and watching over his people. The lonely and weary traveler is made aware of the nearness and reality of God in a place where he does not expect to find him. The divine ministers of mercy are ever attending our way—even though not always perceived—making our requests and desires known unto God, and returning to us with the divine blessing. Centuries later, Jesus sees in this vision of Jacob a clear portrayal of his work and mission here on earth (John 1:51). Jesus Christ himself is the true ladder between God and man. Because God became man and dwelt among us in Christ, we have access through him to the throne of grace where we may receive mercy and find grace to help in time of need (Heb. 4:16).

At the top of the "ladder" which Jacob sees in his vision, the Lord appears and addresses him with words of encouragement and hope. The divine promise of land and numerous seed, which had been made to Abraham (13:15-16) and Isaac (26:3-4), is renewed to Jacob (28:13-14) with special consideration for his present situation: "Behold, I am with you and will keep you wherever you go, and will bring you back to this land; for I will not leave you until I have done that of which I have spoken to you" (28:15). As in the case of Abraham in Egypt and

Isaac in Gerar, God's protective power is here described as
extending beyond the borders of Canaan into Syria.

Jacob awakes from his dream and is afraid, because he senses
the presence of God in this place. Instead of rejoicing in the
comforting promise that God will be with him throughout his
long sojourn away from home, he stands back in fear and cries,
"How awesome is this place! This is none other than the house
of God, and this is the gate of heaven" (28:17). With a kind
of dutiful formality, Jacob "took the stone which he had put
under his head and set it up for a pillar and poured oil on the
top of it" (28:18). A sacred, upright stone, which usually
stood beside an altar, was one of the distinguishing marks of a
sacred place in ancient Israel. Jacob then calls this site Bethel,
that is, the house of God, in commemoration of the Lord's
appearance to him at this spot.

How little Jacob realizes the spiritual significance of this
manifestation of God is shown by the vow which he makes.
Instead of responding to the revelation of God's goodness with
a loving, trustful heart, Jacob bargains with God, making sure
that he will give nothing away until he gets everything that he
wants. God's promises, which should have inspired faith and
trust, are turned into conditions by Jacob—"*If* God will be with
me, and will keep me in this way that I go, and will give me
bread to eat and clothing to wear, so that I come again to my
father's house in peace, *then* the LORD shall by my God, and
this stone, which I have set up for a pillar, shall be God's house;
and of all that thou givest me I will give the tenth to thee"
(28:20-22). Jacob, the bargainer, stoops so low that he bargains
with the Almighty himself. But God does not want Jacob's sacred pillar or his tenths; he wants Jacob. It is not until God
breaks the proud and willful Jacob by the stream Jabbok that
he finally wins him (see Gen. 32). Many times the God we want
is not like the God who wants us.

Jacob Marries Leah and Rachel (29:1-30) [J, E, P]

Jacob finally comes to the "land of the people of the east"
(29:1), another name for Haran (27:43) and Paddan-aram
(28:5). He meets some shepherds with their flocks waiting
beside a well, which is covered with a stone to protect the water
from the rays of the sun and from pollution. We are told that
all these shepherds watered their sheep at the same time, since

the stone that covered the well was so large that it had to be removed by united effort. Jacob learns that these shepherds are from Haran and that they know Laban, his uncle. As they are talking, Rachel comes to the well with her sheep. Anxious to speak with her alone, when he finds out who she is, Jacob suggests to the shepherds that they water their sheep and then take them out to pasture. But they refuse, because not all of their group are present. Jacob, attracted by Rachel's beauty and pleased with his good fortune at finding his relatives so easily, hastens to offer his services to the young damsel in order to make a good impression upon her. Disregarding the rules of the shepherds, Jacob, with Herculean strength, removes the stone from the mouth of the well by himself and waters the flocks of Laban, his mother's brother. Overjoyed at the happy outcome of his journey, Jacob kisses Rachel and cries aloud. When Laban hears that his sister's son, Jacob, has come, he runs out to meet him and welcomes him to his house, where Jacob stays for a month (29:14).

Then things begin to change. Laban, who probably discovers that Jacob is a good shepherd, would like to have him work for him, but since he is a relative, he is not sure of the basis on which he should hire him. This problem is soon solved. Jacob offers to work for Laban seven years without wages, if at the end of that time he may take Rachel as his wife. Laban could not very well turn down an offer like that, and so "Jacob served seven years for Rachel, and they seemed to him but a few days because of the love he had for her" (29:20). Now comes the time when the deceiver is deceived. Jacob, who has run roughshod over everyone who stood in his way, now meets his match. Laban was a sly, avaricious (see 24:29-31), completely unscrupulous man, as his dealings with Jacob well show. The clash of these two kindred souls and their struggle for supremacy forms one of the more exciting chapters in the patriarchal history.

Laban's first chance to practice his treachery on his nephew came on Jacob's wedding night. Taking advantage of the darkness of the evening and the customary veil which enveloped the bride, Laban brings Leah, his first-born and less attractive daughter, to Jacob, who takes her for his wife, thinking of course that it is his beloved Rachel. Laban's flimsy excuse for his deceitful action (29:26) is really not necessary, since Jacob cannot do anything about his marriage to Leah. If the custom of giving the first-born daughter in marriage before the younger actually prevailed in the region, Laban should have informed Jacob, a stranger, about it. Laban now proposes that when the week's marriage festivities for Leah are over, Jacob shall take Rachel for his second wife, on condition that he serve Laban another seven years. Jacob has no alternative, but must accept this proposal, and he takes Rachel as his wife a week after marrying Leah. To have gotten rid of the "weak-eyed" Leah for a handsome price, and to have retained the services of Jacob for another seven years, was a master stroke of craftiness.

The Birth and Naming of Jacob's Children (29:31—30:24) [J, E]

This section contains the list of eleven sons and one daughter born to Jacob while he was in Paddan-aram. The etymologies of the names, for the most part, are based on the rivalry between Jacob's two wives, Leah and Rachel. The fact that all of Jacob's children except Benjamin (see 35:18) were born outside of Canaan may indicate the tradition that the tribal divisions of Israel existed before the occupation of the Promised Land. To discuss fully the etymology of each of these names is beyond the scope of this work. Suffice it to say that for the most part these are purely popular etymologies which are based on resemblances of sound and not on linguistic principles.

"When the LORD saw that Leah was hated, he opened her womb; but Rachel was barren" (29:31). God comforts and blesses the despised wife Leah by opening her womb so that she can have children. To her are born Reuben, Simeon, Levi, and Judah (29:32-35). God therefore overrules the trickery of Laban to his own glory, since Judah is born of Leah. Both David and Jesus are descendants of Leah. So deeply is the divine purpose of salvation woven into the affairs of human life!

Rachel, who can have no children, is envious of her sister. When she petulantly reproaches Jacob for her childlessness, he becomes angry and says, "Am I in the place of God, who has withheld from you the fruit of the womb?" (30:2; see 50:19). God is the source of life and he alone is able to grant such a request. The barrenness of Rachel should be compared with that of Sarah and Rebekah (16:1; 25:21). The continuation of the line of the history of salvation depends entirely upon God (see 18:14). Rachel, in desperation, gives Bilhah, her handmaid, to Jacob so that she "may have children through her" (30:3).

This custom, as we have seen (16:3), was in accordance with the law of the land. By asking Bilhah to bear the children upon her knees, Rachel is expressing the desire to adopt the children of her handmaid as her own. Bilhah has two sons, Dan and Naphtali, who become the adopted children of Rachel. Leah, after her childbearing days are over, also gives to Jacob her maid Zilpah, who bears to him Gad and Asher (30:9-13).

The rivalry between Leah and Rachel continues, with Leah apparently neglected by Jacob, and Rachel still unable to have children. One day Reuben, now a young lad, finds some mandrakes in a wheat field and brings them home to his mother Leah. From early times this herb was believed to have magical properties which promoted conception. When Rachel sees the mandrakes she asks Leah if she may have some of them. Leah at first indignantly refuses, but when Rachel promises to give her husband back to her that night, Leah gives her the supposedly potent herbs. Leah bears two sons, Issachar and Zebulun, and one daughter, Dinah. The writer does not indicate that Leah's renewed fertility is due to the mandrakes, but simply says that God hearkened to Leah and she gave birth to the children (30:17-21). With Rachel, however, the writer is more sure. He states emphatically that it was because of divine intervention that Rachel bore her first son. "Then God remembered Rachel, and God hearkened to her and opened her womb" (30:22). At long last Rachel bears a son. She calls his name Joseph, meaning "God has taken away my reproach" (30:23). According to another tradition she calls his name Joseph, saying, "May the LORD add to me another son!" (30:24).

Jacob Outwits Laban (30:25-43) [J]

Jacob, having served Laban fourteen years, is now anxious to go back to his own country and people. He asks his father-in-law for permission to take his wives and children with him so that he may provide for his own family in his own land. Laban, who knows a good thing when he sees it, is loath to let Jacob go. He confesses that he has been blessed because of Jacob's presence (30:27), so he promises to pay him anything he wants if he will stay. To Laban's amazement, Jacob replies, "You shall not give me anything" (30:31). He asks simply to stay on as a shepherd of Laban's flocks, and to take as his wages "every speckled and spotted sheep and every black lamb, and the spot-

ted and speckled among the goats" (30:32). Later we learn
that the offspring of these animals are also to go to Jacob. Since
most sheep are white and most goats are dark colored or black,
it would appear that Laban has the better of the bargain. To
make his advantage even more secure, Laban separates, by a
three days' journey, the speckled flock of Jacob from his own
normally colored animals, so that Jacob's lesser number will
not be increased by the commingling of the two flocks. Jacob
is left to tend Laban's large flock of white sheep and black
goats, whereas Laban puts his sons in charge of the small flock
of speckled animals which belong to Jacob. At this stage of the
maneuvering Laban seems to have the upper hand; but Jacob still
knows a few tricks which will tip the balance in his favor.

First he prepares streaked rods by peeling strips of the bark,
thus leaving alternate dark and light stripes. These he places
in the watering troughs where the flocks come to drink. Since
the flocks are in the habit of breeding when they come to drink,
they mate with the striped rods before their eyes, which was
thought to cause the ewes to produce offspring similarly striped or
speckled. This meant that the flocks of white sheep and black
goats would bring forth "striped, speckled, and spotted" (30:39).
Verse 40 of this account seems inconsistent with verses 35-36
where we learned that Laban had already removed the multi-
colored animals a three days' journey from the flocks tended by
Jacob. It may be a fragment of an alternate account of the story,
or the account could involve a lapse of time. Since Jacob is in
charge of the large flock of Laban, he will have a large number
of streaked and speckled animals. By still another stratagem Jacob
plans to outwit Laban. He puts the striped rods in the troughs
only when the strongest of the flocks are breeding (30:41-42). In
this way he will keep on getting stronger animals, whereas Laban
will be getting the feebler ones, since they will keep on inbreeding
among themselves. Thus Jacob's possessions increase and he becomes an exceedingly rich man.

Jacob's Flight (31:1-21) [E]

Because of Jacob's rapidly accumulating wealth, Laban's sons
become jealous, and Laban himself no longer looks kindly
upon Jacob. Jacob's decision to leave this unhappy situation
and return to his home is sanctioned by a divine communication
in which the Lord says, "Return to the land of your fathers and to

your kindred, and I will be with you" (31:3; see 28:15). Jacob takes his wives into his confidence and explains to them why he is going to leave Laban and go back home (31:4-13). First of all he informs them of their father's changed attitude toward him. Then he tells them how their father had cheated him, actually changing his wages ten different times, no doubt always to his own advantage, and giving him the spotted and striped animals of the flocks which were always less in number than the normally colored ones. Yet God had been with Jacob for he made the flocks to bear spotted and striped offspring in compensation for the way Laban had treated him. This is quite a different story from the one found in chapter 30, where the spotted and striped young were born as the result of Jacob's clever stratagem, though the two accounts are not necessarily contradictory. The differences are to be explained by the fact that we have here two different textual traditions, the one in chapter 30 being J, the one in chapter 31 being E. It is interesting to note that Jacob is consistently portrayed in a favorable light in the E document. Finally, Jacob reports to his wives that the God of Bethel (see 28: 10-22) has appeared to him and commanded him to go forth from this land and return to the land of his birth.

Jacob's masterful discourse falls upon receptive ears. His wives are willing to leave their father and go with Jacob. Having been treated by their father like foreigners (31:15), that is, like those who occupy inferior social positions, and having been defrauded by their father of money that rightfully belonged to them—Laban had taken all the profits of Jacob's fourteen years of service for himself and had given his daughters no part of it— Rachel and Leah have no qualms of conscience about breaking their home ties and starting life in a new land with their husband. Jacob selects as an opportune moment for their flight the time when Laban is away from home, shearing the sheep. Taking all of the livestock which he had acquired in Paddan-aram, Jacob "fled with all that he had, and arose and crossed the Euphrates, and set his face toward the hill country of Gilead" (31:21). It is also stated in 31:19 that "Rachel stole her father's household gods" (Hebrew, "teraphim"). This was a serious matter, since, according to new evidence from Nuzu, possession of these idols implied leadership of the family. This, no doubt, is the reason why Laban is so concerned about the teraphim when later he overtakes Jacob and his family (31:32-35).

The Meeting of Laban and Jacob (31:22-54) [E, J]

When Laban learns that Jacob has fled with his family and flocks, he pursues him into the hill country of Gilead which is on the east side of the Jordan. On the way Laban has a dream in which God warns him not to say anything to Jacob, implying, of course, that he should not do any harm to the fugitive (31:24). When Laban finally overtakes Jacob he rebukes him severely for stealing away with his daughters as though they were captives of war, and denying him the opportunity of sending his family off with the usual festivities and a farewell kiss (31:27-28). Laban's observation that Jacob has done foolishly is no mere jest. It is a serious matter for Jacob to disrupt the family ties in this way. As Laban says later on, "The daughters are my daughters, the children are my children, the flocks are my flocks, and all that you see is mine" (31:43). Whatever Jacob's precise legal relationship to Laban may have been—he certainly was not a slave, neither had he been legally adopted by Laban according to the narrative as we have it now—he had no right to override the patriarchal authority of Laban by running away with members of his household.

Laban at this moment has not only the right but also the power to punish Jacob for his misdeed, but he is restrained from doing so by the divine command which came to him in a dream. He is determined, however, to retrieve his household idols, which Rachel had stolen without Jacob's knowledge. His frenzied search for these stolen objects is now understood more clearly in the light of the literary remains from Nuzu mentioned above. An adopted son took possession of the idols upon the death of his adopter, but if the adopter had sons of his own after he had adopted a son, the idols passed over to their hands. Thus Jacob has no right to the idols since Laban has sons who must have been born after Jacob's coming to Haran (see 31:41 and 1). Rachel, however, saves the day for Jacob by some clever thinking, and Laban fails to find the idols (31:34-35). The fact that a woman in her condition (see Lev. 15:19) sits upon the idols shows the contempt with which Israel regarded the man-made images of pagan gods (see Isa. 44:9-20).

The tables are now turned. Jacob, who is emboldened by Laban's failure to find the teraphim, upbraids his father-in-law for treating him so miserably over the past twenty years

(31:36-42). He has been an ideal shepherd, always solicitous for his master's interests and unconcerned about his own personal comfort, yet "if the God of my father, the God of Abraham and the Fear of Isaac, had not been on my side, surely now you would have sent me away empty-handed" (31:42). Laban says nothing to defend himself against Jacob's accusations. Claiming his patriarchal control over his family and all their flocks, Laban now suggests that the argument be closed and that a covenant of peace be made between them.

The account of the making of the covenant (31:44-54) is composed of two different sources, J and E, as the repetitions in the story indicate. Two sacred monuments are erected—one a sacred stone (vs. 45), the other a heap of stones (vs. 46); two names are explained—Gilead, from two Hebrew words meaning "the heap of witnesses," and Mizpah, which means a "place of watching," or "outlook post"; the covenant meal is mentioned twice (vss. 46 and 54); and twice God is called as a witness (vss. 49 and 53). But most important of all, the basic terms of the two covenants are entirely different. In one, the rights of Laban's daughters are protected (vss. 49 and 50), and in the other, Laban and Jacob agree to respect the boundary line set up between them and marked by a heap of stones (vs. 52).

When Laban insists in his agreement with Jacob regarding the welfare of his daughters that Jacob is not to take any other wives besides his daughters, he is simply asking Jacob to abide by the laws of the land, for in the literary material from Nuzu it is specifically stated that if an adopted son takes another wife besides the daughter of his adopted father he forfeits the land and buildings which he has inherited. The agreement concerning the border line between Laban and Jacob probably reflects an ancient treaty which established the territorial claims between the Hebrews and their Aramean neighbors to the north.

It is clearly seen in this context that the so-called Mizpah benediction (31:49), which is recited as a parting blessing at many church gatherings, is actually a warning. God's presence is invoked to watch over the two parties of the covenant lest either one should violate his part of the agreement, the inference being that God will punish the offender. This idea of a covenant relation between two parties, described here in a human situation, is later used by Israel's religious leaders to describe the close relationship between God and Israel (see Exod. 19-24).

Jacob Prepares to Meet Esau (31:55—32:23) [J, E]

After Laban kisses his family farewell and departs for Haran, Jacob proceeds on his way and is met by a host of angels. When Jacob sees them he says, "This is God's army!" (32:2). The site where this occurred is accordingly called Mahanaim, which means "two camps." It is situated east of the Jordan River, near the Jabbok, and in later times figures rather prominently in the history of Israel (II Sam. 2:8-32; 17:24-29). What the meaning of this episode is for Jacob himself we are not told. Are these heavenly hosts the guardians of the Holy Land? Are they here to oppose Jacob's entry or to protect him? Or is this the fragment of an ancient story of Jacob's conflict with some heavenly beings, somewhat similar to the struggle described in 32:24-29? It would appear that by manifesting himself to Jacob at this critical moment, God is assuring him of his continued presence and protection (see 28:15) as he enters the Promised Land and prepares to meet his brother. In II Kings 6:15-17 a similar vision of the heavenly hosts is granted to Elisha's servant to assure him of God's presence and protection.

Jacob's first task, as he enters Canaan, is to make things right with his brother, Esau, who had vowed to kill him (27:41). Jacob sends him a most conciliatory message, describing his own great wealth and expressing the desire that Esau will receive him peaceably (32:3-5). The messengers return with word that Esau is already on the way to meet Jacob with four hundred men. Greatly distressed at this news, Jacob does two things. He first of all divides his company into two groups, "thinking, 'If Esau comes to the one company and destroys it, then the company which is left will escape'" (32:8). And secondly, he prays to God for deliverance (32:9-12). This is a remarkable prayer for Jacob to pray. It is not couched in poetic or formally religious terms, but is the spontaneous expression of a heart that is full of fear and anxiety. It shows that in spite of his long record of deceitful actions Jacob has not lost contact with God. After a solemn invocation he reminds the Lord of the promise to bring him back safely to his country and kindred, and he acknowledges his unworthiness in the light of the Lord's goodness to him. He then prays for deliverance from the hand of Esau and for the fulfillment of the Covenant promise. This is truly one of the high points of Jacob's life. The fact that Jacob can and does express his need of God prepares the reader for Jacob's dramatic conversion.

After his prayer, Jacob makes last-minute preparations to meet Esau (32:13-23). First of all, he selects a sizeable number of animals from his herds as a present for Esau. He then decides to have his servants present the animals to Esau in successive droves, with a considerable space between the droves. By this show of generosity Jacob hopes to break down Esau's resentment against him. "I may appease him with the present that goes before me, and afterwards I shall see his face; perhaps he will accept me" (32:20). Finally, as a precaution against a surprise attack, Jacob sends his family and flocks across the Jabbok, the modern Zerqa, under cover of night, while he remains behind alone.

God Wrestles with Jacob (32:24-32) [J]

"And a man wrestled with him until the breaking of the day" (32:24b). Jacob, left alone in the dark night, is afraid of what the morrow will bring forth. Memories of the wrongs he has done to Esau crowd in upon him and his conscience is sorely troubled. His real battle, however, is with God, not with Esau. He must make things right with God before he can face Esau and make things right with him. At this moment, in the dead of night, when resistance is the lowest and Jacob is alone with his fears and stricken with remorse, "a man" lays hold upon him and wrestles with him until the break of day.

Who this nocturnal visitor is we are not told. The indefinite term "man" allows for any number of interpretations. Jacob, according to the biblical account, realizes that his antagonist is a supernatural being (32:25), a god in human form, whom he identifies as God himself (32:30). Hosea calls the assailant an angel, who was overcome by Jacob's tears and supplication (Hosea 12:3-4). Luther sees in the "man" an appearance of the preincarnate Christ, who "showed Himself to the fathers in such form as would indicate that He would sometime dwell with us on earth in the flesh and in human form." Whoever we may think the "man" in this verse is, the biblical writer believes that Yahweh, the God of Israel, is dealing directly and personally with Jacob to change his life and to give him a new name. It is primarily God who is wrestling with Jacob, not Jacob with God. God initiates the struggle, which ends in the defeat of the old Jacob. It is God who "touched the hollow of his thigh" (32:25) and made him helpless. It is God who breaks the stubborn, willful, self-reliant Jacob and brings him to his senses. But from verse 26 on it is Jacob who does the fighting—or, perhaps better, the clinging—until he receives the blessing. Physically broken and crippled, Jacob's only weapon now is God's word of promise. "I will not let you go, unless you bless me" (32:26). He who had promised to do Jacob good (32:12) cannot break away until he has blessed Jacob.

The blessing which Jacob receives is a new name, Israel, which has been translated "he who strives with God" (see 32:28, margin), but which, more accurately, means "God strives," or, "may God strive." In either case, the new name commemorates the night of struggle which was the turning point in Jacob's life. The new man receives a new name. The heavenly visitor, on the other hand, refuses to reveal his own name (32:29; see Judges 13:18 for a similar concealment of the divine name). The site of Penuel (also known as Peniel), which means "face of God," is said to have derived its name from this incident, for Jacob said, "I have seen God face to face, and yet my life is preserved" (32:30). The belief that a person died when he saw God is expressed in several passages in the Old Testament (see Exod. 33:20; Judges 6:22-23). Yet Jacob had seen God and lived. Triumphant, yet humbled, Jacob limps along in the light of the rising sun, carrying in his body the scar of his conversion (32:31).

Jacob Meets Esau (33:1-20) [J]

The dreaded moment has finally come when Jacob is to meet Esau face to face. The sight of Esau approaching with four hundred men revives Jacob's fears. "So he divided the children among Leah and Rachel and the two maids. And he put the maids with their children in front, then Leah with her children, and Rachel and Joseph last of all" (33:1-2), so that, in case of attack, those most dearly loved by Jacob would have the best chance of escape. As the head of his household, Jacob leads the way into the presence of Esau, bowing respectfully seven times. In contrast with this formality, Esau runs to meet Jacob, embraces him, falls on his neck and kisses him. After the whole family politely bows before Esau and is introduced, Jacob urges Esau to accept his gift of flocks as a further proof of his friendliness toward him. After accepting Jacob's gift, Esau suggests that they journey together with his men serving as a bodyguard for Jacob's party through the rough and dangerous land of Seir. Jacob, however, politely refuses to travel with Esau, but he does say that he will follow at a slower pace behind him until he meets him in Seir. Esau then sets out for his homeland to the south, and we hear of him no more. But Jacob, contrary to his word, moves westward toward the Jordan Valley and stops at Succoth. Esau, pictured in this chapter as a noble and chivalrous character, forgives and forgets his brother's past wrongdoings. Jacob, however, still a little mistrustful of the one whom he had betrayed, gives Esau the slip by going toward Canaan instead of following him to Seir as he had promised.

The last three verses of the chapter tell of Jacob's safe arrival at Shechem, in the center of Canaan, where he buys a piece of land and erects an altar to El-El'ohe-Israel, which means, "God, the God of Israel." This purchase was historically important, for here Joseph's bones were buried (Joshua 24:32; see Acts 7:16), and here was situated the well of Jacob where Jesus conversed with the woman from Sychar (John 4:6).

The Sons of Jacob Take Shechem (34:1-31) [J, E]

This ancient story, in terms of personal history, tells about the conquest of Shechem, in central Canaan, by the Israelites. Jacob, who plays a very weak role in the whole affair, represents the Israelites who are living in central Palestine; Simeon and Levi, who take the leading part in subduing the Shechemites and rescuing their sister Dinah, represent the two conquering Israelite tribes, whose violent action is later repudiated by the nation (34:30; 49:5-7). There seem to have been two different accounts of the episode, usually attributed to J and E, although an exact literary analysis of the passage eludes us. The action begins when Dinah, the daughter of Leah (30:21), is seized and dishonored by Shechem, the son of Hamor. When the sons of Jacob hear what has happened to their sister, they are very angry, "for such a thing ought not to be done" (34:7). The strong language of reprobation used here has a religious background, for the bitter hatred of Dinah's brothers for Shechem represents Israel's hatred for the Canaanites and their sexual religious rites. That which has occurred is a sacrilege and it must be avenged immediately and thoroughly. There could be no compromise between Israel and her neighbors on this score.

After the ravishing of Dinah, Shechem, according to one account, promises to pay Jacob and his sons any amount as a marriage gift if he may marry the maid (34:11-12). Hamor, the father of Shechem, however, wants to negotiate for bigger stakes. "The soul of my son Shechem longs for your daughter; I pray you, give her to him in marriage. Make marriages with us; give your daughters to us, and take our daughters for yourselves. You shall dwell with us; and the land shall be open to you; dwell and trade in it, and get property in it" (34:8-10). What Hamor is suggesting here is a union of the two groups on the basis of intermarriage, trade, and the right to settle in the land. Jacob would obviously benefit more from Hamor's proposed union than the Shechemites would, probably as compensation for the offense done to his daughter. The sons of Jacob ostensibly accede to Hamor's proposal, on condition that all of the male citizens of Shechem be circumcised (34:13-17). It is implied here that the Canaanite dwellers in Shechem did not practice circumcision, whereas the custom was prevalent among the Hebrews from earliest times. Using this ancient rite as a ruse, the Israelites plan to wipe out the male population of the city when they are powerless to defend themselves.

The proposal of the sons of Jacob is acceptable to Hamor and Shechem, who now must sell the idea to the townspeople (34:18-24). They persuade their fellow citizens to accept the terms of the Israelites, noting diplomatically the advantages which the group will derive, rather than their own personal gain. On the third day after the rite of circumcision was performed on the men of Shechem, Simeon and Levi, the full brothers of Dinah, enter the city, kill all the males, and take their sister out of Shechem's house (34:25-26). According to 34:27-28, all the sons of Jacob plunder the city and take everything as their booty. Jacob timidly scolds his sons because they have brought trouble upon him, but the writer seems to condone the act by allowing the sons the last word. It is quite possible that Jacob's harsher words against Simeon and Levi in 49:5-7 refer to this treacherous deed. At any rate, both Simeon and Levi are later dislodged from Shechem, Simeon finding refuge in the southern part of Judah, and the tribe of Levi being scattered among the other tribes of Israel. It was to Shechem that Joshua called the tribes to hear his farewell address and to renew the Covenant (Joshua 24), and here it was that the ten tribes, after rejecting Rehoboam, made Jeroboam their king (I Kings 12:1-20). It became the first capital of the Northern Kingdom (I Kings 12:25).

Jacob Returns to Bethel (35:1-29) [E, P, J]

God's command to Jacob to go up to Bethel rounds out the story of Jacob's association with this religious site. The vow which Jacob had made there when he was fleeing from Esau (28:20-22) is now to be fulfilled. The verb "go up" to Bethel (vss. 1 and 3) is used here in the sense of making a pilgrimage to a sacred spot (see I Sam. 1:3; Ps. 122:4). In preparation for the pilgrimage to the place where the God of his fathers had appeared to him, Jacob orders his household and retinue to give him their idols and superstitious objects so that he may bury them, for anything belonging to a strange god would be taboo at the holy place of the God of Israel. The people also purify themselves with ceremonial washings and change their clothes as a sign of their inward renewal before God (see Joshua 24:23).

On their journey to Bethel, God protects his people from contamination with the Canaanites by causing a mighty fear to fall upon the cities of the land, and the people are not molested (35:5). This mysterious terror was similar, no doubt, to the holy fear that sometimes fell upon Israel's enemies in battle and caused them to panic (see Joshua 10:10).

When Jacob comes to Bethel, which was formerly called Luz, he builds an altar and calls the place "El-bethel," that is, the God of Bethel. Here God appears to him and changes his name to Israel and renews the blessing of numerous seed and the Promised Land which he had bestowed upon Abraham and Isaac. After this appearance Jacob sets up a sacred pillar and pours a libation of oil upon it. This is P's theological summary of the events described in 28:10-22 (J, E) and 32:23-32 (J).

The rest of this chapter contains fragmentary notices from the Jacob tradition. In verses 16-21 the birth of Benjamin and the death of Rachel are recorded. On the way from Bethel to Ephrath (perhaps Parah in the territory of Benjamin; see Joshua 18:23), Rachel gives birth to a son, whom she names in her dying moments Ben-oni, that is, "son of my sorrow." His father, refusing to let his son bear such an unlucky name through life, renames him Benjamin, which means "son of the right hand," or, "child of good luck." Ephrath is later identified with Bethlehem, which is in Judah (vs. 19; see, however, I Sam. 10:2, where Rachel's tomb is said to be in the territory of Benjamin). With the notice of Reuben's act of incest in verse 22, compare Genesis

49:3-4. Isaac dies in Hebron and is buried in the cave of Machpelah. Esau and Jacob attend his burial, just as Isaac and Ishmael attended the burial of Abraham (25:9).

The Descendants of Esau (36:1-43) [P]

The appropriate place for the list of Esau's descendants is between the notice of Isaac's death (35:29) and the story of Jacob's family (37:2). Esau, the rejected one, now steps aside and the Chosen People begin to play their all-important role in redemptive history. The chapter is composed of six main lists of names, with certain additional material: verses 1-8, 9-14, 15-19, 20-30, 31-39, 40-43. Of these, verses 1-8, 9-14, 15-19, and 40-43 preserve the basic records of the family of Esau, or, in the formal expression of Genesis, the "generations" of Esau.

Verses 20-30 contain the genealogies of the Horites, or, more accurately, the Hurrians, who were the original inhabitants of the land of Seir. They were a non-Semitic people who had spread so widely over the Canaanite lands of Syria and Palestine in the second millennium that one of the Egyptian names for Canaan was *Khūru*, a word related to "Hurrian."

The king list in verses 31-39 shows that the Edomite monarchy was in existence "before any king reigned over the Israelites." These kings of Edom do not belong to a dynasty, but are represented as coming from different cities. In this respect they were like the judges of Israel, or even like Saul, Israel's first king, who was not much more than a tribal chieftain. It is only because of Israel's great interest in the movements of history and in the history of the peoples surrounding her land that records like these have been preserved. It is from Israelite sources alone that we derive our knowledge of the Edomites.

The Joseph Story (37:1—50:26) [J, E, P]

The Joseph story is quite different from the other patriarchal narratives. Its clearly conceived plot, well-delineated character studies, and highly developed style of composition are in sharp contrast with the loosely connected accounts of the patriarchs in the preceding chapters of Genesis. It is the finest example of the *"novelle,"* or "novelistic" type of literary composition in the Old Testament. Joseph, the hero of the story, is idealized more than any other patriarchal character. His biography is given in such great detail that we know more about him than about any other character in the Old Testament, with the possible exception of David. He is a model son, a perfect servant, and an ideal administrator. His character is exemplary, he is poised and self-assured as he stands before men of authority, and above all, he has an unshakable faith in God which helps him to overcome all difficulties. The basic theme of the whole story is best expressed in Joseph's own words to his brethren: "As for you, you meant evil against me; but God meant it for good, to bring it about that many people should be kept alive, as they are today" (50:20; see also Ps. 105:17-23 and Acts 7:9-16). His faultless character and absolute trust in God stamp him as the ideal man in Hebrew history, pointing beyond himself to the One who was altogether perfect, and, who, by his perfect obedience, brought salvation to the whole world.

Although there are indications that the text of the Joseph story as we have it passed through the hands of J, E, and P, the literary excellence, the unity of structure, and the movement of the "plot" seem to indicate that the story was originally conceived and written down by a single author. The writer was well acquainted with Egyptian customs and institutions (for example, see 43:32; 47:13-26; 50:2-4), and the story of Joseph's encounter with Potiphar's wife (ch. 39) is closely paralleled in an old Egyptian tale called "The Story of Two Brothers." Other striking parallels to the Joseph narrative have recently been discovered in inscriptional material from Syria, dating from the fifteenth century B.C. The similarity of these literary remains points to a long literary history of the Hebrew story of Joseph before its incorporation into the patriarchal history of Genesis.

Joseph Hated by His Brothers (37:1-36)

Although the following chapters deal with the history of Joseph, they are introduced by the phrase, "This is the history of the family of Jacob" (37:2). The reason for this caption is that Jacob is recognized as the head of the family until his death (49:33), and whatever happens to his immediate sons while he lives is regarded as part of the history of Jacob. There are three reasons given at the beginning of the story which explain Joseph's unpopularity with his brothers. First of all, the sons of Jacob's concubines, Bilhah and Zilpah, are naturally jealous of Joseph, the son of Jacob's wife Rachel; and the fact that he

brings bad reports concerning them to his father does not help
to make the situation any better. In addition to this, Israel rather
unwisely shows his favoritism for Joseph by making him a long
robe with sleeves. This robe (literally, "a tunic of palms or
soles") differed from the ordinary tunic in that it extended to
the palms of the hands and the soles of the feet. The Septuagint
calls it "a coat of many colors." The same Hebrew expression is
used to describe the dress worn by the daughter of David (II
Sam. 13:18).

Finally, the brothers are especially incensed when Joseph
relates to them two dreams in which he is represented as being
superior to them, as well as to his father and mother (so 37:10,
but Rachel had already died, according to 35:19). In the first
dream, when Joseph and his brothers are binding sheaves in the
field, Joseph's sheaf arises and stands above the others, which
bow down in obeisance to his sheaf. In the other dream the
sun, moon, and eleven stars bow down to Joseph. The meaning
of these dreams is perfectly clear to his brothers and his father
without any special interpretation. In spite of the jealousy of
his brothers and the rebuke of his father, Joseph is destined to
rise to a position of superiority over his family. The double
dream indicates the certainty of fulfillment. The course of Joseph's whole life is set by this early revelation of his ultimate
triumph over seemingly insurmountable obstacles to become
the savior of many people (50:20).

The embittered brothers soon find a way, as they think, to
dispose of this dreamer of dreams. Israel sends Joseph to inquire
about the welfare of his brothers who are tending their father's
flocks near Shechem. When they see him afar off they conspire
to kill him. "Here comes this dreamer," they say. "Come now,
let us kill him and throw him into one of the pits; then we shall
say that a wild beast has devoured him, and we shall see what
will become of his dreams" (37:19-20). It is obviously more
than jealousy that is driving the brothers to this heinous deed.
"The master of dreams" (according to the Hebrew in 37:19)
has certain insights and powers which they cannot understand,
and they are fearful that his dreams will be realized. Therefore
they think that they have to kill him in order to make sure that
his dreams will never come true. When they first lay hands on
Joseph to kill him, Reuben, the oldest brother and therefore the
most sensible, pleads for his life, and he is spared. They strip

Joseph of his robe with sleeves and throw him into a pit that has no water in it. When a caravan of Ishmaelite merchants comes by, Judah, pleading for his brother's life, suggests that they sell him to the Ishmaelites. In this way his life will be spared and the brothers will be free of his blood.

There seem to have been two different traditions regarding Joseph's fate which have been woven together in the present account. In one (37:25-27, 28b), the brothers sell Joseph to the Ishmaelites for twenty shekels of silver, about two-thirds of the value of a full-grown slave, and therefore adequate for a youth like Joseph (see Lev. 27:5 and Exod. 21:32), and he is taken down into Egypt. According to the other (37:28a, 29-30), Midianite traders pass by, and while the brothers are eating, kidnap Joseph from the pit and carry him to Egypt (see 40:15, where Joseph refers to this version of the story). Reuben returns to the pit and finds to his dismay that it is empty.

The treacherous character of the brothers is further emphasized by the way they deceive their aged father, Jacob. When he is led by their cruel stratagem to believe that Joseph is dead, he mourns bitterly for his son many days. Sheol, according to Old Testament teaching, is an underground place of shadowy existence. The last verse in the chapter prepares us for the story in chapter 39. So Jacob, who himself betrayed his father Isaac and robbed the brother whom his father dearly loved, is betrayed by his sons and is made to believe that he has lost his favorite son. In the sufferings of Israel the heavy hand of God's judgment is seen.

Judah and Tamar (38:1-30)

Two chapters, 38 and 49, appear to be inserted into the Joseph narrative. Chapter 38, the Judah-Tamar episode, is out of context and probably belongs to a tradition quite independent of the Joseph story, since Judah is represented as being separated from his brethren and settled permanently in southern Palestine. Chapter 49, which recounts the patriarchal blessing upon the sons of Jacob, is probably included because it contains the words of blessing bestowed upon Joseph and his descendants. But the question still remains, Why was the Judah-Tamar story inserted at this particular place in the Joseph narrative, between chapters 37 and 39? One answer given is that at this point there is a logical break in the story, since Joseph has disappeared from the scene so far as his father and brothers are concerned, and is ready to take up his new life in Egypt. It is probable, however, that there may have been a more basic reason for inserting the story of Judah and Tamar at this place. In the chapter (39) that follows we are told how Joseph is tempted by Potiphar's wife. No one can read that dramatic scene without feeling utter contempt for the Egyptian temptress. She is the example, par excellence, of the wicked woman who lures young men to their doom by her wily charms and slippery words (see Prov. 7). Tamar, on the other hand, is the ideal wife in Israel who will try anything to give her deceased husband progeny so that his name may be preserved. The writer expresses no surprise at Tamar's actions, nor does he censure her for tricking her father-in-law into giving her a child. She is doing her duty as a loyal wife in gaining seed for her dead husband and maintaining the family honor. Could it be, then, that these two stories were set side by side in order to contrast the ideal wife in Israel with the wicked Egyptian wife of Potiphar?

The opening eleven verses of the chapter give the background of the story. Judah separates himself from his brothers and dwells among the Canaanites in Adullam, several miles southwest of Jerusalem. Here he marries a Canaanite woman and she bears three sons to him—Er, Onan, and Shelah. He then takes a Canaanite woman, by the name of Tamar, as a wife for his first-born, Er, who dies soon after marriage, without progeny. Judah then gives his second son Onan to Tamar to raise up seed to her deceased husband (see Deut. 25:5-10), but he refuses to fulfill his duty and is slain by the Lord. Judah does not give his youngest son, Shelah, to Tamar, lest he suffer the same fate as his brothers. He conceals his real purpose for withholding Shelah by pretending that he is too young to take a wife. Then Judah sends Tamar back to her father's house, in accordance with the law for a childless widow (Lev. 22:13).

Judah's own wife now dies, and Tamar devises a plan to make him perform the duty of her husband's brother. She puts off her widow's garments and, veiling herself like a prostitute, sits by the side of the road along which, she hears, Judah is coming, "for she saw that Shelah was grown up, and she had not been given to him in marriage" (38:14b). Judah, seeing her by the roadside, and thinking because of her veiled face that she is a prostitute (see Prov. 7:10), asks to go in unto her, not knowing of course that she is his daughter-in-law. The price he offers to pay is a kid from the flock, which he promises to send to her. Now comes the master stroke of Tamar's plot. She asks him to give her a pledge until he sends her the kid. When he asks her what pledge she wants, she immediately replies, "Your signet and your cord, and your staff that is in your hand" (38:18). These were personal belongings which made absolutely certain the identification of the owner. The cord was probably used to suspend the signet ring around the neck. "So he gave them to her, and went in to her, and she conceived by him" (38:18c).

Three months later Judah is told that Tamar, his daughter-in-law, has played the harlot and is pregnant. Judah, as the head of the family, sentences her to death by burning. Usually the penalty for adultery was stoning (see Ezek. 16:38-40; John 8:5), although burning alive is mentioned as the punishment of a priest's daughter who plays the harlot (Lev. 21:9). Burning is probably the older form of punishment. When Tamar is brought out to receive her punishment, she dramatically announces that whoever owns the signet, cord, and staff which she has in her possession is the father of the child. Judah admits that he is the owner, and acknowledges that he is guilty in that he has failed to observe the marriage customs of the land. "She is more righteous than I, inasmuch as I did not give her to my son Shelah" (38:26).

To us the trickery of Tamar may seem entirely wrong and disgusting, but we must judge her action in the light of conditions which prevailed thousands of years ago. We should remember that many of the marriage customs described in the early books of the Bible are the social expressions of man's basic urge to survive in the face of a hostile world. That the writer of the story in no way condemns Tamar is truly significant, but that she should be especially honored by appearing among the names of the ancestors of the Messiah on the first page of the New Testament is even more remarkable (Matt. 1:3).

As the last verses of this chapter indicate, the immediate purpose of the story is to explain the origin of two divisions of the tribe of Judah, namely, the families or clans of Perez and Zerah (38:27-30; see also Num. 26:20).

Joseph and Potiphar's Wife (39:1-23)

In Egypt Joseph becomes the slave of Potiphar, an officer of Pharaoh. He is put in charge of his master's house and he manages it with unusual success. Joseph is quite different from any other slave Potiphar has ever owned. Instead of being surly and difficult to handle, like most slaves, Joseph is obedient, honest, and completely reliable. How is this to be explained? The writer now introduces the main theme of the whole Joseph narrative, and he does so with such a flourish that the reader cannot avoid getting the point. Within the scope of four verses (39:2-5) the writer tells us five times that it is the Lord who is the cause of Joseph's success. "The LORD was with Joseph, and he became a successful man . . . and his master saw that the LORD was with him, and that the LORD caused all that he did to prosper in his hands. . . . From the time that he made him overseer in his house and over all that he had the LORD blessed the Egyptian's house for Joseph's sake; the blessing of the LORD was upon all that he had, in house and field." The unbelievable cruelty of the brothers, the anguish of Jacob's broken heart, the utter loneliness and misery of a young boy far from home, fade out of view as we see Joseph enjoying his newly acquired success. In the overruling providence of God the sorrows of life and the sins of wicked men are made to serve the divine purpose of redemptive grace. "The LORD was with Joseph" is the key to this magnificent story. We also see that the man of God is a source of blessing to those around him.

"Now Joseph was handsome and good-looking" (39:6b). This sentence prepares us for the events which follow. Potiphar's wife, who is enamored of the handsome new house slave, tries to seduce him, but without success. He parries her advances by declaring that he cannot betray the trust which his master has placed in him, and he cannot sin against God (39:9). By sinning against man Joseph feels that he is sinning against God. The fact that Joseph is at all times conscious of God's presence makes every sin an action against God (see Ps. 51:4). His every action is controlled by God's moral law. This is the first time in the record of Israel's history that a man deliberately sets obedience to God's laws above the gratification of his own passions, even though it may have been to his own advantage to be in the good graces of his master's wife. Because of this victory over temptation, Joseph has become the model of conduct for every young man to emulate, the ideal character of the Old Testament, foreshadowing the perfect life of Israel's greater Son.

When Potiphar's wife is unable to entice Joseph, she brings a false charge against him, first before the servants of the house, and then before her husband, who casts him into prison. Once again, as in a great symphony, the theme is sounded in strong, clear words: "But the LORD was with Joseph and showed him steadfast love, and gave him favor in the sight of the keeper of the prison. And the keeper of the prison . . . paid no heed to anything that was in Joseph's care, because the LORD was with him; and whatever he did, the LORD made it prosper" (39:21-23). Joseph's certain knowledge that the Lord is with him in prison gives him courage to endure the most severe of his trials, and inspires him to lead an exemplary life in the face of a seemingly hopeless situation (see Ps. 105:18-19).

Joseph Interprets the Dreams of the Butler and the Baker (40:1-23)

Some time after Joseph has been cast into prison the butler and baker of the king of Egypt are taken into custody because they have in some way offended their lord, and they are placed in the same prison with Joseph while their case is being investigated. The captain of the guard appoints Joseph to care for his new charges until their fate is decided.

One night both the butler and the baker dream, "each his own dream, and each dream with its own meaning" (40:5b). When Joseph comes to them the next morning, he sees that they are troubled. "Why are your faces downcast today?" he asks; and they reply, "We have had dreams, and there is no one to interpret them." Then Joseph says to them, "Do not interpretations belong to God? Tell them to me, I pray you" (40:7-8). Here a new idea is added to the dream motif in the Joseph narrative. In the first brace of dreams in which Joseph's future was foretold (37:5-10), the meaning of the dreams was ascertained by both Jacob and his sons without an interpreter. Now Joseph claims that the interpretation of dreams belongs to God. Interpretation of dreams is not a science which can be learned, nor an occult art which can be practiced by magical means, as the Egyptians believed. According to the Hebrew view, God alone knows the future, and the man to whom God reveals his secrets is the only one who can interpret them. This view is also expressed in Daniel 2:28, 47; 4:18, where the dream motif is largely patterned on that which is found in the Joseph narrative. Upon hearing the dreams, Joseph correctly interprets them, as future events soon prove. The butler is restored to his former position, but the baker is hanged. Joseph's request of the butler, to mention him to Pharaoh when he gets out of prison, is forgotten for the moment (40:14, 23). But later his ability as an interpreter of dreams is remembered, and he successfully interprets the dreams of Pharaoh himself.

Joseph Interprets Pharaoh's Dreams (41:1-57)

For two long years after the execution of the baker, Joseph languishes in prison, being tested by the word of the Lord (see Ps. 105:19). Then Pharaoh has two wonderful dreams which his wise men cannot interpret. In the one dream, seven lean cows eat up seven sleek and fat cows, and in the other, seven thin and blighted ears of grain swallow up seven plump and full ears. When Pharaoh awakes he is troubled, for he is quite sure that a pair of dreams which are so similar must have some special significance. He calls together the magicians and wise men of Egypt to interpret the dreams, but they are unable to solve the mystery of their meaning.

At this critical moment the chief butler remembers the young Hebrew in prison, who had correctly interpreted his dream and the dream of the chief baker two years before. He describes the incident to Pharaoh, who is so impressed that he summons Joseph to come before him. After shaving himself, according to the custom of the Egyptians, and changing his clothes, Joseph is hastily brought into the presence of the king of Egypt. Pharaoh tells Joseph that he has had a dream which no one can interpret, and expresses the hope that Joseph will be able to determine its meaning. Joseph, in his usual calm and fearless manner, says to Pharaoh, "It is not in me; God will give Pharaoh a favorable answer" (41:16). Pharaoh thinks that Joseph is just another magician, who uses his special knowledge and techniques to divine the future, but Joseph quickly tells him that he has nothing to do with it (literally, "not unto me") and that God is the One who will give the interpretation.

Pharaoh then recounts his dreams to Joseph, who immediately interprets them with clarity and ease. "The dream of Pharaoh is one; God has revealed to Pharaoh what he is about to do" (41:25). There will be seven years of plenty in Egypt, followed by seven years of famine, and the doubling of the dream "means that the thing is fixed by God, and God will shortly bring it to pass" (41:32). After interpreting the dreams Joseph calmly goes on to offer some practical advice about preparing for the impending crisis. He suggests that a food administrator—"a man discreet and wise" (41:33)—should be selected and set over the land of Egypt, and that overseers should be appointed throughout Egypt to store up one-fifth of the produce of the land during the seven plenteous years as a reserve against the seven years of famine.

It will be noted that God is not only the interpreter of Pharaoh's dreams through the special powers he gives to Joseph, but he also is the One who gives the dreams in order to reveal what is about to take place (41:25, 28). One may detect, therefore, a studied development in the dream motif of the Joseph narrative. The first two dreams (ch. 37) are symbolic, and need no interpreter, for their meaning is clear. In the second brace of dreams (ch. 40) God alone is the One who can give the interpretation. In the last two dreams (ch. 41) God is not only the source of the interpretation, but also the One who gives the dreams in order to reveal to Pharaoh the approaching years of famine. It is theologically significant that these events in the life and history of Egypt are determined by the eternal purpose of God, and come to pass according to his holy will (41:32).

Pharaoh heartily agrees with Joseph's practical suggestion for dealing with the imminent crisis, and appoints Joseph as the chief administrator of the government's food conservation program. Joseph is second only to Pharaoh himself in the whole land of Egypt. He receives from the king his own personal signet ring, the symbol of his newly acquired power and authority. He is dressed in the finery of Egypt, and is made to ride in the second chariot, next to Pharaoh's. When he passes by, the people shout, "Abrek," a word of uncertain meaning (see footnote to 41:43). It obviously expresses the respect of the people for a high official in the land. As a final gesture of good will, Pharaoh gives him an Egyptian wife by the name of Asenath, the daughter of Potiphera, priest of On (that is, Heliopolis, a few miles to the north and east of modern Cairo) (41:45). Joseph's long years of trial and tribulation are finally crowned with success. God's holy purpose is at long last fulfilled in the life of Joseph for the salvation of his people.

Joseph is thirty years old when he enters the service of the
king of Egypt (41:46). Having come to Egypt when he was
seventeen (37:2), Joseph has spent thirteen years in servitude
in the land. After the years of plenty, during which Joseph has
stored up enormous quantities of grain, the years of famine
come upon Egypt and surrounding lands, so that all the earth
comes to Joseph to buy grain (41:53-57). With this statement
the writer prepares us for the events which follow in the story.

In the names of Joseph's two sons, Manasseh and Ephraim,
whose births are recorded in this chapter (41:50-52), the two
parts of Joseph's life are remembered. "Joseph called the name
of the first-born Manasseh, 'For,' he said, 'God has made me
forget all my hardship and all my father's house.' " From the
time Joseph had left Canaan until he stood before Pharaoh, he
had known only the most heartbreaking experiences and the bit-
terest disappointments. Yet God, in his mercy, had wiped them
out of his memory and filled his mind with holy thoughts. His success as food administrator in Egypt is recalled in the name of
Ephraim, his second son, which is interpreted to mean, "For God
has made me *fruitful* in the land of my affliction."

The First Journey of Joseph's Brothers to Egypt (42:1-38)

With this chapter we come to the second part of the Joseph
narrative, which deals specifically with Joseph and his brethren.
In the narrative, which has some elements of the typical success
story, the hero not only triumphs over all odds to reach the
pinnacle of success, but he also succeeds against the efforts of all
who have tried to impede his inevitable rise to fame and glory.
Of course, in the religious tradition of Israel, any idea of revenge is greatly tempered, for vengeance belongs to God (see
50:19), and Joseph sees the overruling hand of God working
against the evil machinations of his brethren (50:20). To be sure,
in the beginning, it appears that Joseph lords it over his brethren
and plays with them as a cat plays with a mouse. They are entirely at his mercy and he can do anything he wants with them.
But behind this show of seeming unconcern for the hapless
victims, the writer is constantly letting the true character of the
hero shine through. Joseph's interest in Benjamin and Jacob and
his emotional struggles as he meets his brethren from time to
time prepare the reader for the high moment of reconciliation
which will come in due course.

In chapter 42 the first meeting between Joseph and his brethren is described. The reader is taken back to Canaan once again,
to the home of Jacob and his sons. There is a famine in the land
and Jacob tells his sons to go down to Egypt to buy grain that
they may live (see also 12:10). The brothers go down to Egypt
without Benjamin, whom Jacob refuses to send, and are brought
before Joseph, the governor of the land. He recognizes them as
they bow down before him (see 37:7, 9) and immediately accuses them of being spies. This they stoutly deny, citing their
family connections as evidence of their good intentions. Joseph
takes advantage of this unsolicited information and demands
that Benjamin, their youngest brother, be brought to Egypt
before they may return home.

After being imprisoned for three days, the brothers are again
brought before Joseph, who now makes a more moderate proposal. One of the brothers shall remain confined in prison (in
42:16, one brother was to be sent for Benjamin and the rest
were to remain in Egypt) while the others return home with the
grain and bring their youngest brother back again to Egypt.
The words, "and they did so" (42:20), are out of place in their
present context. These harsh demands of Joseph remind the
brothers of their heinous crime which they had committed
against their brother years before, and they make common
confession of their guilt to one another (42:21). They now
realize that the "distress" which they had brought upon their
brother (his pitiful plea for mercy, recorded here, is not mentioned in the account of the happenings in chapter 37) is now being
meted out to them. This is the first step in the theology of reconciliation. The offenders must first come to the place where they
acknowledge that they have done wrong and where they are
sorry for their sins. The true character of Joseph breaks through
his stern exterior when he turns away and weeps as his brothers
(not knowing, of course, that he could understand their whole
conversation) confess their sins before him (42:23-24).

In accordance with Joseph's second proposal, Simeon is chosen
to remain behind in prison until the brothers return wth Benjamin. On the way home the brothers stop off at a lodging place
for the night and find, to their dismay and discomfiture, that the
money which they paid to Joseph for the grain had been put
back into their bags (42:26-28; 43:21; see 42:35, where it is
said that they find the money when they reach home). Their cry

of consternation, "What is this that God has done to us?" reveals their common fear that God's judgment is continuing to be visited upon them. When Jacob learns of Simeon's fate in Egypt he accuses his sons of taking both Joseph and Simeon from him, thus unwittingly increasing their sense of guilt. In spite of Reuben's offer of his two sons as a pledge for Benjamin's return the sorrowing patriarch refuses to let them take Benjamin back to Egypt, since he is the only surviving son of his beloved Rachel (42: 36-38).

The Second Visit to Egypt (43:1-34)

The famine continues to be severe in Canaan, and Jacob now has to decide whether he and his family will starve, or whether he will part with his son Benjamin. This time it is Judah who recounts what had happened to the brothers in Egypt (42:29-34), re-emphasizing the demand of the Egyptian official, who of course is Joseph, that they bring their youngest brother back with them if they want permission to buy grain. In Judah's speech nothing is said of Simeon, who, according to 42:24, was left behind in Egypt. When Judah offers his own life as a pledge for Benjamin's safety (43:9), Jacob yields to his sons' demands and allows Benjamin to return with them to Egypt. With typical shrewdness, Jacob also suggests that they take a present to the Egyptian official—some choice fruits of the land, and the money which had been found in their bags—"perhaps it was an oversight" (43:12). (For the meaning of "God Almighty," see the discussion of 17:1.) "So the men took the present, and they took double the money with them, and Benjamin; and they arose and went down to Egypt, and stood before Joseph" (43:15).

When the brothers reach Egypt they appear before Joseph to carry on the business for which they have come. Joseph, upon seeing Benjamin, is so overjoyed that he orders a banquet to be prepared for his brothers in his private residence. This lavish display of kindness makes them suspicious that Joseph is setting some kind of trap for them, because of the money that was replaced in their bags the first time. Therefore, before they enter the house of Joseph, they tell the steward about the discovery of the money in their bags and explain that it had been returned to them entirely without their knowledge. He assures them that they need not fear, because he himself had received the money from them in payment for the grain. They should, therefore, ascribe their good fortune to their God and the God of their father, who must have mysteriously put the money in their bags (43:23). Since an Egyptian steward would hardly know anything about the God of these foreign Israelites, we may surmise that Joseph had instructed him what to say. The release of Simeon is noted here, although up to this point in the chapter the brothers have said nothing about Simeon's retention in Egypt.

After making themselves ready for the meal, the brothers bring their present to Joseph and bow down before him (see 37:7, 9). He inquires about the welfare of his father, and is moved to tears when he sees his youngest brother, Benjamin (see 42:24). After gaining control of himself again, he invites them all to sit down and eat. According to the custom of the land, Joseph sits apart from his brethren, "because the Egyptians might not eat bread with the Hebrews, for that is an abomination to the Egyptians" (43:32). The brothers are amazed when they see that they are seated in the order of their seniority. How could anyone in Egypt have known their ages? They are further mystified by the special attention paid to Benjamin, who is served five times more food than the rest of them. So tension mounts! The writer, with profound insight into the psychology of human nature, is skillfully preparing the reader for the climactic moment of reconciliation.

The Final Testing of the Brothers (44:1-34)

Joseph now makes arrangements with his steward to test the sincerity of his brethren for the last time. Not only is the money which the brothers had paid for their grain put back into their bags as before, but Joseph's own silver drinking cup is put into Benjamin's bag. After the brothers leave the city, Joseph orders his steward to follow them. When he has overtaken them, he is to accuse them of stealing his lord's most cherished possession, the silver cup from which he drinks and which he uses for divining the future. The problem of reconciling Joseph's sincere faith in the God of his fathers with the assumption that he practiced the pagan rite of divination is passed over by the writer without comment. Information about the future was obtained from the divining cup by throwing fragmentary objects into it and observing either the arrangement into which they fell, or the motion of the liquid which they caused when thrown into the cup.

When the steward overtakes the brothers and accuses them of the theft, they stoutly deny the charge, and propose death for the thief and slavery for the rest of them if the missing cup should be found in one of their bags. The steward, offering easier terms —the thief alone shall be enslaved—starts searching their bags, "beginning with the eldest and ending with the youngest; and the cup was found in Benjamin's sack" (44:12). Naturally dismayed when the cup is found in their possession, the brothers submissively return to the city, never suspecting that a trick has been played on them. Joseph's practice of divination is again mentioned (44:15). Whether he did actually practice divination, or whether he only wished his brothers to think so, is not clear. Judah can say nothing in defense of himself or his brothers except that God is evidently punishing them for some secret sin they have committed (see 42:21). This statement prepares the way for the full confession of their sin against Joseph in the verses which follow. Judah's proposal that they all remain in Egypt as Joseph's slaves is turned down by Joseph as too severe. He suggests that only Benjamin stay in Egypt as his slave, while the rest of them return to their aged father. By giving them this choice, Joseph is subjecting the brothers to the severest test of all. Will they abandon Benjamin, as they had abandoned Joseph before, or will they refuse to return to Canaan without their brother? The next verses show how they stand the test.

Judah's plea for Benjamin which follows is one of the finest examples of persuasive eloquence in the Old Testament (44:18-34). With singular pathos and beauty Judah describes the aged father's unwillingness to let Benjamin go with his brothers to Egypt for food. Particularly moving is the description of Jacob's feeling for his lost son, Joseph. "You know that my wife bore me two sons; one left me, and I said, Surely he has been torn to pieces; and I have never seen him since. If you take this one also from me, and harm befalls him, you will bring down my gray hairs in sorrow to Sheol" (44:27-29). With these words Judah lays bare before Joseph his brothers' evil deed. The cycle is now complete. Those who once had cruelly torn their young brother from their father's side now confess their guilt before him and plead for mercy. Joseph's strategy has been successful. He has brought his hostile brethren to the point where they acknowledge their sin and look to him for mercy. In the concluding part of his speech, Judah tells how he has made himself personally responsible to Jacob for Benjamin's return (43:9), and so, with remarkable magnanimity, he offers to stay in Egypt as a substitute for Benjamin, in order to spare their father the sorrow of losing his youngest son. There is no question that Joseph's strategy has paid off. He now realizes that his brethren have changed, and that the moment of reconciliation has come.

It is instructive to note the different ways that God uses man's sin in the Joseph narrative to bring about his holy purpose. In the first place, God uses the hatred and jealousy of Joseph's brethren to bring him to Egypt and to eventual success. Man's evil designs cannot thwart God's well-laid plans; more often they contribute to the accomplishment of the divine purpose. In the second place, God uses man's sin to prove and purify his saints. Joseph's faith was severely tested by the wickedness of his brethren and by Potiphar's wife, but he did not fail. In the third place, God uses man's sin to convict him of his guilt and show him his need of forgiveness. When Joseph's brothers realize the heinousness of their crime, they readily confess and beg Joseph's forgiveness.

Joseph Reveals Himself to His Brothers (45:1-28)

Overcome by Judah's moving plea for Benjamin, and convinced at last of his brothers' changed character, Joseph makes himself known to them. Having dismissed his attendants so that he might be alone with his brethren at this tense moment, Joseph breaks down with loud weeping and says, "I am Joseph; is my father still alive?" (45:3). This seems to be a strange question to ask after the preceding conversations, yet it is one which Joseph might naturally ask under emotional strain, since his father's welfare is uppermost in his mind. So dismayed are the brethren at the disclosure of Joseph's identity that they stand speechless in his presence. He tries to allay their fears in words that reveal the basic philosophy of his life. "God sent me before you to preserve for you a remnant on earth, and to keep alive for you many survivors. So it was not you who sent me here, but God; and he has made me a father to Pharaoh, and lord of all his house and ruler over all the land of Egypt" (45:7-8). Three times in this section—twice in the verses just quoted and once before in verse 5—Joseph ascribes the reason for his success to divine providence: "God sent me before you to preserve life." God overruled their crime to make Joseph the preserver of life.

The words "survivors" and "remnant" (45:7) have strong theological overtones which should not be ignored. In the Flood story, Noah is snatched from the waters of destruction by God's grace to start a new branch of the human race. Abraham is separated from his family ties in order that he may become a blessing to all men. And Joseph sees in his own personal experience how he was providentially delivered from the hands of evil men in order to save his people from destruction. The "remnant" in this context probably refers to the family's descendants. The fulfillment of God's promises to Abraham, Isaac, and Jacob (see 50: 24) is assured because by God's grace Joseph is alive and able to dispense life-giving bread to his brothers and their children. In this miraculous way the Chosen People are preserved to carry God's blessings to future generations. The phrase, "a father to Pharaoh" (45:8), is probably an honorary title given to a good administrator in Pharaoh's government.

Joseph bids his brothers go back to Canaan and tell their father how God had made him lord of all Egypt. "You must tell my father of all my splendor in Egypt, and of all that you have seen" (45:13a). He also invites them all to return to Egypt and dwell in the land of Goshen, a fertile region in the northeast Delta section of Egypt (see 47:11). The fact that Joseph says that they will then be near him (45:10) indicates that the court of Pharaoh was not far from Goshen. Historically this situation fits best into the Hyksos period of Egyptian history when the Egyptian capital was in Avaris (later known as Tanis), a city in the Delta area. The Hyksos were a foreign people—the word means, "rulers of foreign lands"—mostly of Canaanite stock, who invaded Egypt and ruled over the land from about 1710 to 1550 B.C. Immediately before and after the Hyksos period the Egyptian Pharaohs used as their capital the city of Thebes in Upper Egypt. Therefore, if Joseph says that he will be near his people when they are in Goshen, he is most probably serving in the court of a Pharaoh whose capital is in Lower Egypt, the Delta region of the Nile. This and other evidence—for example, the 430 years' sojourn in Egypt (Exod. 12:40) added to the generally accepted date of the Exodus, shortly after 1300 B.C.—points to the conclusion that Joseph came into power in Egypt somewhere around 1700 B.C.

Pharaoh likewise invites Joseph's brethren and their father to come to Egypt and settle in the best part of the land (45:16-20). He even offers to send wagons to Canaan to transport the women and children on the long journey back to Egypt.

Joseph sends his brethren back to Canaan, laden with gifts,

and he exhorts them not to quarrel among themselves by the way (see 42:22). He is afraid that the disclosure of his identity may stir up new conflicts among them and jeopardize his plans for bringing the family down to Egypt. When Jacob hears that Joseph is still alive he becomes numb, "for he did not believe them" (45:26). When he sees the wagons which Joseph had sent to carry them back to Egypt his spirit quickly revives, and he is ready at once to go and see his son before he dies.

Jacob Goes Down to Egypt (46:1—47:12)

From this point on to the end of the book (chs. 46-50) the Joseph story takes on more of the coloring of the earlier patriarchal narratives. We hear again of visions in the night, manifestations of God at religious sites, patriarchal blessings, and the promise of the land which God had sworn to Abraham, Isaac, and Jacob. In fact, these chapters deal mainly with the last acts of Jacob. After hearing that Joseph is still alive Jacob sets out, presumably from Hebron (see 37:14), and journeys to Beer-sheba, the sanctuary which is particularly associated with Isaac (see 26:23-25; 28:10; but also 21:31-33). Here he offers "sacrifices to the God of his father Isaac" (46:1) in order, no doubt, to obtain divine approval to go down to Egypt (see 26:2, where it is stated that Isaac was not allowed to journey to Egypt). God appears to Jacob in visions of the night and divine approval is obtained for the journey. "I am God, the God of your father; do not be afraid to go down to Egypt; for I will there make of you a great nation. I will go down with you to Egypt, and I will also bring you up again; and Joseph's hand shall close your eyes" (46:3-4). The "God of the fathers" protects the patriarchs whether they are in Egypt, Syria, Gerar, or Canaan. The divine promise to bring Jacob up again to Canaan refers no doubt to the Exodus, though Jacob's body is returned there for burial (50:4-13). Assured of divine protection on the journey, Jacob leaves Beer-sheba and finally arrives in Egypt with his family and their possessions.

Now follows a list of "the names of the descendants of Israel, who came into Egypt" (46:8-26), which breaks the thread of the story. Actually this may be more accurately described as a list of Jacob's descendants rather than a record of those who went down to Egypt with Jacob, since it includes Joseph and his sons (46:20). A similar list, with certain variations and expansions, occurs in Numbers 26 and I Chronicles 2-8.

The third part of this chapter (46:28-34) resumes the narrative begun in the opening verses. The reason for sending Judah ahead of the company is not clear according to the Hebrew text. Perhaps the rendering of the Revised Standard Version is best here, according to which Judah is sent ahead to arrange for Joseph's meeting with Jacob. With great haste Joseph rides up to Goshen to meet his father whom he has not seen for over twenty years. The dramatic union is filled with deep emotion as Joseph falls on his father's neck and weeps "a good while" (46:29). After this touching scene Joseph prepares Jacob and the brothers for their audience with Pharaoh. Joseph will return to Pharaoh and tell him that they have come with their possessions, including their flocks and herds. When Pharaoh calls them and asks, "What is your occupation?" they are to answer, "Your servants have been keepers of cattle from our youth even until now, both we and our fathers" (46:33-34). They are to answer Pharaoh in this way so that he will give them the land of Goshen to dwell in.

Why the writer closes the chapter with the notice that "every shepherd is an abomination to the Egyptians" is not clear. Nowhere in Egyptian literature has this statement been confirmed, although there is evidence that swineherds and cowherds were looked down upon by the Egyptians. It is strange that if shepherds were so thoroughly despised they would be given the best pastureland in the country (see 47:6). Perhaps what is reflected in these words is the Egyptians' hatred for the Asiatic nomads who were continually infiltrating into Egypt from the north. Yet, in spite of this hatred, Pharaoh allows Joseph's family to settle in Goshen. God, by his wisdom and power, can even overrule the prejudices of Pharaoh and his people so that his saving purpose may be realized in the history of Israel.

The audience with Pharaoh turns out as expected. Joseph presents five brothers to the king, who inquires about their occupation. When he learns that they are shepherds (47:3; see 46:34, where they are told to say that they are "keepers of cattle"), he gives them the best of the land, Goshen, to dwell in, and as an additional favor he offers to put the most capable of Joseph's brothers in charge of the royal herds. Then we are told that Joseph presents his father to Pharaoh, who, being impressed with the appearance of the aged patriarch, inquires first as to his age (47:7-8). He replies: "The days of the years of my sojourning are a hundred and thirty years; few and evil have been the days of the years of my life, and they have not attained to the days of the years of the life of my fathers in the days of their sojourning" (47:9). In comparison with his fathers, Jacob's life has been shorter and harder. Abraham had died when he was 175 years old (25:7), and Isaac at the age of 180 (35:28). And there is no question that Jacob appeared to have more than his share of troubles in the course of his life—his flight from home as a lad, his strife with Laban, the loss of his beloved wife Rachel and of his favorite son Joseph, and the violence of Simeon and Levi.

"The land of Rameses" (47:11), another name for the land of Goshen, is no doubt so called from the city of Rameses (see Exod. 1:11) which was built by Rameses II (1290-1224 B.C.), the probable Pharaoh of the Exodus. The description of this region in Joseph's time (about 1700 B.C.) as the land of Rameses would therefore be an anachronism (see chapter 26, where the term "Philistines" is an anachronism).

Joseph's Policies as Food Administrator (47:13-27)

This is a rather remarkable passage in that it deals almost exclusively with Egyptian affairs. We hear nothing about Joseph's relation to his brothers or to his father, Jacob, or about their settlement in the land of Goshen. The passage would appear to fit in better with the closing verses of chapter 41 than with the material that immediately precedes it. There seem to be three phases in Joseph's policy of distributing food during the devastating famine in Egypt. At first, the money of the people is accepted in exchange for food (see 41:57), vast wealth being accumulated in the royal coffers (47:14). After the people's money is exhausted, Joseph orders them to give their cattle in payment for food (47:16-17). How the royal herdsmen can handle all the cattle of Egypt is not discussed. After the people give up all their cattle, they suggest that they sell themselves with their land in slavery to Pharaoh in return for food and seed to sow the land (47:19, 23). The reference here to seed for sowing the land would seem to indicate that the famine is now over, and the regulations for land tenure seem to presuppose normal conditions, rather than times of famine. The crown naturally accepts these generous terms of the people, who become at once, with the exception of the priests, both slaves and tenants of the Pharaoh, paying him annually a land tax of twenty per cent of the produce. The people seem content with their new lot. "And they said, 'You have saved our lives; may it please my lord, we will be slaves to Pharaoh' " (47:25).

Jacob's Last Acts; He Blesses Ephraim and Manasseh (47:28—48:22)

Jacob's age, at the time of his death, is one hundred and forty-seven years. His request to be buried in Canaan is recorded in 47:29-31 (J) and in 49:29-32 (P). According to this tradition he makes Joseph swear to him that he will not bury him in Egypt. Joseph promises to comply with Jacob's wishes and pledges his oath by placing his hand under his father's thigh (see 24:2-9). Later on Joseph has to ask Pharaoh's permission to carry out Jacob's request (50:4-6). Jacob's bowing himself upon the head of his bed is probably to be interpreted as an act of worship, expressing gratitude to God for granting his last wish (47:31b).

Although it has already been noted that Joseph promised Jacob on his deathbed to bury him in Canaan—47:29-31 (J)—it appears from 48:1, which must belong to another tradition (E), that Joseph learns here of his father's illness for the first time. He thereupon brings his two sons, Manasseh and Ephraim, to his father to receive the patriarchal blessing. Summoning his strength to sit up in bed, Jacob reminisces about God's appearance to him at Bethel (35:11-12), where he received the divine promise of numerous descendants and the land of Canaan as his possession. In view of these promises Jacob now adopts Joseph's two sons, Ephraim and Manasseh, who were born in Egypt, into the family and gives them the same status as Reuben and Simeon, Jacob's two eldest sons. Any other children of Joseph and their descendants shall belong to either Ephraim or Manasseh (48:5-6). On Jacob's sad reference to Rachel's death, see 35:16-19. The relation of this verse (48:7) to its context is not clear.

Verse 8 seems to resume the thread which was interrupted by Jacob's description of the appearance at Bethel (48:3-4). The two sons are introduced to Jacob, whose eyes are dim with age. As they draw near to him he greets them with a kiss and embraces them, rejoicing that now he has seen not only Joseph but his children as well. "Then Joseph removed them from his knees, and he bowed himself with his face to the earth" (48:12). Evidently the rite of adoption is referred to here, but not fully described. Ephraim and Manasseh may have sat on or between their grandfather's knees, symbolizing their acceptance into the family (see 30:3), after which Joseph removes them. Then Joseph leads the brothers, Ephraim in his right hand and Manasseh in his left, toward Jacob, thinking that Manasseh, the older, would receive the richer blessing from Jacob's right hand. Jacob, however, crosses his hands and puts his right hand with the more powerful blessing upon Ephraim, the younger son, and his left hand upon Manasseh. The idea of the younger son eclipsing the older seems to be a favorite biblical theme, as, for example, Jacob and Esau, Joseph and his brothers, David and his brothers.

The blessing which follows is divided into two parts: 48:15-16 and 48:20. "And he blessed Joseph, and said:

> 'The God before whom my fathers Abraham and Isaac walked,
> the God who has led me all my life long to this day,
> the angel who has redeemed me from all evil, bless the lads;
> and in them let my name be perpetuated, and the name of my
>   fathers Abraham and Isaac;
> and let them grow into a multitude in the midst of the earth' "
>   (48:15-16).

According to these words, Jacob blesses Joseph in the words he pronounces upon Ephraim and Manasseh.

The threefold invocation is most impressive and inspiring. First, Jacob calls upon the God of the fathers before whom they had walked in their pilgrimage on earth (17:1; 24:40). Then he invokes God, the Shepherd, who has led him all through life to this day. The figure is particularly appropriate in the mouth of Jacob, the shepherd (see chapter 30). The English translation misses the point completely, for "who has led me" is literally "who has shepherded me." The figure of God, the Shepherd, is found throughout the Scriptures (49:24; Ps. 23:1; Isa. 40:11; John 10:11-16). Thirdly, Jacob calls upon the Redeemer God who, by his Angel, has delivered him from all evil (31:11; 32:1, 24-30). Although the term "redeem" is used here in the sense of deliverance from physical danger and calamity, later passages of Scripture use it in the theological sense of redemption from sin (see Isa. 44:22-23; 63:9; Ps. 103:4). God is called the Kinsman-Redeemer of Israel in Isaiah 44:24; 49:7. (For the duties of the kinsman-redeemer in Israel, see Leviticus 25:48-49; Deuteronomy 25:5-10; Ruth 3:13; 4:6; Jeremiah 32:6-15.) After the invocation, Jacob prays that his name and the names of Abraham and Isaac may be perpetuated in Joseph's two sons, thus making

Ephraim and Manasseh full members of the family of Israel.

Joseph objects to having Jacob's right hand upon Ephraim, the younger, and his left hand upon Manasseh, the older, and so he tries to reverse the order, but Jacob, with prophetic insight, declares that he has acted correctly, since Ephraim shall be greater than Manasseh (see Num. 1:33, 35; 2:19, 21). This order is then sanctioned by the word of blessing which follows (48:20). Jacob concludes his patriarchal blessing by predicting that his descendants will return again to Canaan, and by declaring that Joseph shall possess "one mountain slope which I took from the hand of the Amorites with my sword and with my bow" (48:22). The obvious reference here is to Shechem (the word for "mountain slope" and the name Shechem are similar in sound), which is given as a special gift to Joseph and his descendants. Joseph is said to have been buried at Shechem (Joshua 24:32). The warlike conquest of Shechem is quite a different picture from that described in chapter 34, where Jacob is said to have disapproved of Shechem's destruction by his sons (vs. 30), and to have departed to dwell elsewhere. According to 33:18-19, Jacob came in peace to Shechem and purchased a plot of ground there.

The Blessing of Jacob (49:1-27)

The main section of this chapter (vss. 3-27) is composed of a group of ancient oracles, written in poetic form, which describe the characters and fortunes of the twelve tribes of Israel. In 49:1-2, serving as the introduction to the passage, these utterances are characterized as predictions, addressed by Jacob to his sons as they are gathered around his deathbed. In 49:28, on the other hand, we are told that they are blessings which Jacob pronounced upon the twelve tribes of Israel. How the term "blessing" can be applied to all of the oracles recorded in this chapter is difficult to understand, since Reuben is severely reprimanded for his weakness of character, and Simeon and Levi are actually cursed for their deeds of violence. It is clear after reading through these poems that they are not dealing with the affairs of Jacob's sons as such (see 49:1), but rather with the history of the tribes they represent (see 49:28). They must have been composed long after the time of Jacob, when nationalism was strong in Israel, and the characteristics of the various tribes were well established (see also the lists of tribal oracles found in Judges 5 and Deuteronomy 33 which are similar in many ways to the poem in Genesis 49). The names "Jacob" and "Israel," for instance, used in verses 7 and 16 for the nation, emphasize the national character of the poem. Then, too, the historical and geographical background of the various utterances reflects conditions which prevailed in Israel from the days of the judges to the time of David (see below for detailed discussion). By ascribing these oracles to Jacob, the writer is expressing his conviction that the patriarch, like the prophets of a later age, actually molded the history of God's people by the power of his word, whether it was the word of blessing or the word of judgment. The order of the names of the tribes is given according to the order of the birth of the sons of Jacob as found in Genesis 29, 30, and 35. First come the sons of Leah, then the sons of the concubines, and finally those of Rachel. Within the first two groups a few changes have been made in the order of the sons.

Reuben, the first-born, is full of vitality and excels in pride and power, but he loses his pre-eminent position among his brothers by defiling his father's bed (49:3-4; see 35:22). The early decadence of the tribe of Reuben is noted in the Song of Deborah (Judges 5:16), where it is denounced for its indifference in time of national crisis, and in Deuteronomy 33:6, where it appears to be on the verge of extinction. In the history of Israel the tribe of Reuben was a nonentity—no important person, judge, king, or prophet ever came from Reuben.

Simeon and Levi are cursed by God and punished because of their wanton violence and cruelty (49:5-7; see 34:25). In very early times Simeon was practically absorbed by Judah (compare Joshua 19:1-9 and 15:20, 26-32, 42), and Levi was dispersed throughout the land without territorial possessions. The priestly character of the tribe of Levi is not indicated here (see Deut. 33:8-11).

Judah (49:8-12), whose name is associated with the Hebrew word "to praise" (29:35), receives the praises of his brothers. Judah is like a lion, invincible in battle and secure in his lair (see also Rev. 5:5). Who dares to challenge him to battle? The scepter and the ruler's staff, symbolic of kingly authority, will not pass from Judah "until he comes to whom it belongs," or, according to another translation, "until Shiloh come." In other words, the line of David will continue until a more glorious future is inaugurated with the appearance of the Messiah, to whom the kingdom rightfully belongs.

Many and varied are the interpretations of the difficult Hebrew word *"shīlōh"* in this passage. It is generally accepted that "Shiloh" is not a proper name denoting the Messiah. This translation is based mainly on a vague Talmudic passage. Neither does the word refer to the religious site in central Palestine where the Ark of the Covenant rested during the days of the judges. According to this interpretation the passage would read, "Until he comes to Shiloh." It would be difficult to see why the Davidic Messiah of the tribe of Judah would return to a religious sanctuary in Ephraim which had been destroyed by the Philistines before David even became king. The translation of the Revised Standard Version, which has the support of most early versions, is probably the best. It is interesting to note that the Jewish sect from Qumran by the Dead Sea interpreted this passage messianically. In a fragment which contains a commentary on Genesis 49:10, this phrase is interpreted to mean "Until the Messiah of Righteousness shall come."

The last two verses of the Judah oracle describe the rich vine culture of the land which shall be a sign of the Messianic Age. The One who is to come will be riding upon an ass (see Zech. 9:9), and when he dismounts he will tie his beast to a vine. No Palestinian would ever think of fastening his beast of burden to a vine, for it would quickly strip the plant of its fruit. But in the Messianic Age, even the animals will enjoy the riches of the land. Also the grapes will be so plentiful that the ideal ruler who is to come will be able to wash "his garments in wine and his vesture in the blood of grapes."

The oracle about Zebulun notes the rather remarkable fact that this tribe lives by the sea and is interested in ships (see also Deut. 33:18-19, where both Issachar and Zebulun are made rich by the treasures of sea and sand). The Israelites who dwelt in the interior regions of Canaan never became a maritime people.

The tribe of Issachar (49:14-15), which settled in the southern part of Galilee (Joshua 19:17-23), is chided for living in ease and luxury and becoming enslaved to her Canaanite overlords.

Dan, one of the smallest tribes in Israel, is like a serpent which attacks enemies much larger than itself and destroys them (49:16-18). Dan was able to maintain its independence among the larger tribes of Israel by moving to the northern part of the country (see Judges 1:34; ch. 18). The connection of the last verse of this oracle (vs. 18) with the preceding verses is not clear.

Gad, whose land is east of the Jordan (Joshua 13:8), is able to hold off successfully the bedouin raids from the desert (49:19).

Asher, who resides along the seacoast (Judges 5:17), is blessed with ample food (49:20; see Deut. 33:24).

The meaning of the Naphtali oracle is not clear (49:21). It suggests in a general way that the tribe enjoys the blessings of prosperity (see Deut. 33:23, where this idea is clearly stated).

The oracle concerning Joseph (49:22-26) is the longest and most eloquent in the chapter. The enthusiastic praise of the mighty tribes of Ephraim and Manasseh is even greater than that which is bestowed upon Judah. This poem should be compared with the corresponding section in the Blessing of Moses (Deut. 33:13-17). First, Joseph is described as exceedingly prosperous and populous. He is "a fruitful bough," and "his branches run over the wall." His enemies, antagonized by his great prosperity, attack him fiercely with their bows and arrows, but by God's help he overcomes them. The God who helps Joseph and blesses him so abundantly is given five titles within a few lines, as though to emphasize his great power and beneficence. He is called the Mighty One of Jacob (see Isa. 1:24); the Shepherd (see 48:15); the Rock (literally, the Stone) of Israel (only here, but probably synonymous with the title "Rock" for God, found in Deut. 32:4 and elsewhere); the God of your father (see, for example, 26:24); and God Almighty (see 17:1). The blessing upon Joseph follows. It consists of blessings of the soil (fertility) and of the womb (numerous offspring), and the blessings of the promise given to Jacob, now passed on to Joseph and his descendants.

Benjamin (49:27) is described as a ravenous wolf because of his warlike character (see Judges 5:14; chs. 19-20).

Jacob's Death; the Last Acts of Joseph (49:28—50:26)

In the last verses of chapter 49 we find another account of Jacob's request to be buried in Canaan with his fathers (see 47:29-31). Those already buried in the cave of Machpelah are mentioned—Abraham and Sarah, Isaac and Rebekah, and Leah. Rachel, it will be remembered, was buried a few miles south of Bethel (35:16-20). After finishing his charge to his sons, Jacob "drew up his feet into the bed, and breathed his last, and was gathered to his people" (49:33).

After Jacob's body is embalmed and the seventy days of mourning for him are over, Joseph asks Pharaoh for permission to take his father's body back to Canaan for burial. The request is granted, and the funeral cortege, composed of numerous Egyptian attendants and the family of Jacob, makes its solemn way to Canaan. After Jacob is buried in the cave of Machpelah, Joseph, his brothers, and those who are with them return to Egypt.

Now that their father has died, the brothers feel insecure, for they are completely at the mercy of the one they had wronged. "It may be that Joseph will hate us and pay us back for all the evil which we did to him" (50:15). At first they send a message to Joseph, asking his forgiveness. They strengthen their plea for mercy by appealing to a dying request of their father which has not been mentioned heretofore (50:16-17). Then the brothers come themselves, and, bowing down before Joseph (see 37:7, 9), they offer themselves to him as his slaves. In answering the brothers' pathetic plea, Joseph sounds the keynote of the whole narrative (see also 45:5, 7-8). Joseph says, "Fear not, for am I in the place of God? As for you, you meant evil against me; but God meant it for good . . . that many people should be kept alive, as they are today. So do not fear; I will provide for you and your little ones" (50:19-21a). With self-effacing humility Joseph reminds his brothers that he is not God, and so he has no right to judge or punish them (see Deut. 32:35-36; Heb. 10:30). Above the evil machinations of his brothers was the overruling providence of God. God was actually using their jealous hatred to bring about his saving purpose, "that many people should be kept alive." In this spirit of humility and deep personal faith in the eternal purposes of God, Joseph forgives his brothers and promises them and their families protection and nourishment.

The last act of Joseph's life is filled with prophetic significance. "Then Joseph took an oath of the sons of Israel, saying, 'God will visit you, and you shall carry up my bones from here' " (50:25). By this oath Joseph reaffirms his faith in the God of Israel. He is certain that the end of redemptive history is not "a coffin in Egypt," the last phrase in the Book of Genesis. To be sure, the final consummation of God's plan of redemption is still in the future, but it is assured by men of faith like Joseph.

The prophetic significance of Joseph's last words is not forgotten by succeeding generations, for it is recorded that "Moses took the bones of Joseph with him; for Joseph had solemnly sworn the people of Israel, saying, 'God will visit you; then you must carry my bones with you from here' " (Exod. 13:19). And Joshua, when he enters the land of Canaan, buries the bones of Joseph in Shechem (Joshua 24:32). In Hebrews 11, the roll call of Israel's heroes of faith, this command of Joseph's is singled out as the most significant act of faith in his whole life. "By faith Joseph, at the end of his life, made mention of the exodus of the Israelites and gave directions concerning his burial" (Heb. 11:22).